Florentine Ariosto Jones

A Yankee in Switzerland and the Early Globalization of the American System of Watchmaking

by

Frank Jacob
Nord University, Norway

Series in American History
VERNON PRESS

Copyright © 2022 Vernon Press, an imprint of Vernon Art and Science Inc, on behalf of the author.

All rights reserved. No part of this publication may be reproduced, stored in a retrieval system, or transmitted in any form or by any means, electronic, mechanical, photocopying, recording, or otherwise, without the prior permission of Vernon Art and Science Inc.
www.vernonpress.com

In the Americas:
Vernon Press
1000 N West Street, Suite 1200,
Wilmington, Delaware 19801
United States

In the rest of the world:
Vernon Press
C/Sancti Espiritu 17,
Malaga, 29006
Spain

Series in American History

Library of Congress Control Number: 2021936473

ISBN:

Also available: 978-1-64889-360-5

978-1-64889-289-9 [Hardback, Premium Color]; 978-1-62273-887-8 [Hardback, B&W];

978-1-64889-359-9 [Paperback, Premium Color]; 978-1-64889-309-4 [PDF, E-Book]

Product and company names mentioned in this work are the trademarks of their respective owners. While every care has been taken in preparing this work, neither the authors nor Vernon Art and Science Inc. may be held responsible for any loss or damage caused or alleged to be caused directly or indirectly by the information contained in it.

Every effort has been made to trace all copyright holders, but if any have been inadvertently overlooked the publisher will be pleased to include any necessary credits in any subsequent reprint or edition.

Cover design by Vernon Press.

Cover image: Unidentified soldier, possibly Private Florentine Ariosto Jones of Co. A, 13th Massachusetts Infantry Regiment, in Union uniform with pocket watch. Library of Congress: https://www.loc.gov/pictures/item/2012649879/

Table of contents

List of Figures and Tables   v

Foreword by David R. Seyffer   ix

Introduction   xi

1. A Short History of American Watchmaking until the Civil War   1

2. The Civil War, Jones, and the Birth of an Idea   29

3. Jones and the International Watch Company   45

3.1. The Swiss Context   45

3.2. Jones and His Watch Company   58

3.3. Home Made and Global Problems   73

Conclusion   87

Index   101

List of Figures and Tables

Figures

Fig. X.1: Florentine Ariosto Jones, 1841-1916, IWC Archives.	xiv
Fig. X.2: Jones's signature, IWC Archives.	xv
Fig. X.3: IWC Factory Building, 1883, IWC Archive, P07–1054.	xix
Fig. X.4: Savonnette Pocket Watch showing a Mississippi steamship, 1874, property of Hannes A. Pantli.	xx
Fig. 1.1: Marine chronometer (small longitude clock no. 1), 1777. Photo taken in the Musée des Arts et Métiers by David Monniaux, 2006.	2
Fig. 1.2: Portrait of Jean-Antoine Lépine.	3
Fig. 1.3: Illustration of a Goddard watch from 1812, Pocket Watch Database.	4
Fig. 1.4: The Pitkin watch, 1838.	6
Fig. 1.5: Photograph of the ceremony for the completion of the First Transcontinental Railroad and the driving of the golden spike at Promontory Summit, Utah, May 10, 1869. Samuel S. Montague of the Central Pacific Railroad and Grenville M. Dodge of the Union Pacific Railroad shake hands.	10
Fig. 1.6: A Banjo clock created by Aaron Willard, 1815-1825, Metropolitan Museum of Art, New York, NY.	12
Fig. 1.7: William C. Bond.	14
Fig. 1.8: Atlas with the clock at the Tiffany & Company Building, 727 Fifth Avenue, New York. Courtesy of Tristan Surtel, photo taken by Meg Lessard, June 8, 2014.	15
Fig. 1.9: A clock from Chauncey Jerome's clock company (according to markings inside), presumed 19th century. Photo taken by JVGJ, personal acquaintance of User: Bunchofgrapes, May 31, 2016.	16
Fig. 1.10: Aaron Lufkin Dennison. Portrait from Abbott's *The Watch Factories of America* (1888).	19
Fig. 1.11: Waltham Factory, Boston Watch Company.	22

Fig. 1.12: Movement of a Waltham model 57, photo taken by Bonsairolex, September 10, 2011. 23

Fig. 1.13: E. Howard & Co. Watch Advertisement, 1930. 25

Fig. 1.14: Images from Boss's Patent, 1859, Pocket Watch Database. 27

Fig. 2.1: Unidentified soldier, possibly Private Florentine Ariosto Jones of Co. A, 13th Massachusetts Infantry Regiment, in Union uniform with pocket watch, Library of Congress. 31

Fig. 2.2: 19th-century watch dealer's business card with Elgin logo, Boston Public Library. 33

Fig. 2.3: United States Watch Co., Newark, NJ, Pocket Watch Database. 34

Fig. 2.4: Waltham Watch Co. advertisement, 1890s. 36

Fig. 2.5: The army of the Potomac at Mine Run – General Warren's troops attacking, *Harper's Weekly*, 1 January 1864. 40

Fig. 3.1.1: Frédéric Japy, Frédéric Japy, portrait, Musée Japy, Beaucourt. 48

Fig. 3.1.2: Fritz Zuber-Bühler (1822-1896), The Watchmaker and His Family. 50

Fig. 3.2.1: Monument to Heinrich Moser in Schaffhausen's "Mosergarten" (Moser garden), photo taken by Hauserphoton, April 4, 2020. 61

Fig. 3.2.2: A "Jones calibre," raw movement, serial no. 16688. 66

Fig. 3.2.3: Jones calibre pocket watch, Pattern B, key-wind, ca. 1872. 70

Fig. 3.2.4: Working box used to assemble watches in Jones's factory. IWC Archive, P07-1259. 71

Fig. 3.2.5: IWC pocket watch for women. Only three of them are known to remain worldwide. 73

Fig. 3.2.6: IWC pocket watch for women. Only three of them are known to remain worldwide. 73

Fig. 3.3.1: Half-page IWC advertisement in *The Watchmaker and Jeweller*, May 1873, P06_1893, IWC Archive. 77

Fig. 3.3.2: Schwob Frères advertisement in *The Jewelers' Circular and Horological Review* 5, no. 10, November 16, 1874: 169. 79

Fig. 3.3.3: Schwob Frères advertisement in *The Jewelers' Circular and Horological Review* 6, no. 1, February 1875: 7. 80

Fig. 1: Mount Auburn Cemetery, Cambridge, Massachusetts. Photograph by Frank Jacob. 88

Fig. 2: Mount Auburn Cemetery, Cambridge, Massachusetts. Photograph by Frank Jacob. 89

Fig. 3: Mount Auburn Cemetery, Cambridge, Massachusetts. Photograph by Frank Jacob. Unfortunately unrelated to Florentine A. Jones. 90

Tables

Table 1.1: Clock types and numbers sold by Edward Howard's and Seth Thomas's companies between 1871 and 1911. 8

Table 2.1.: Members initiated into Rheinfall-Lodge No. 9 in 1877/78. 43

Table 3.1: Swiss watch exports to the United States. 56

Table 3.2.1: Types of Jones's ébauches. 67

Table 3.2.2: Estimated number of Jones's movements that were marketed until 1878. 69

Foreword by David R. Seyffer

Biographies are an important field in historical studies for understanding actors and individual actions. However, as a literary genre, they can also bring to life long-gone eras and social structures, especially when scientifically researched and methodically structured. With the book *Florentine Ariosto Jones: A Yankee in Switzerland and the Early Globalization of the American System of Watchmaking*, Frank Jacob brings a delightful and captivating biography of the founder of IWC Schaffhausen, fruitfully counterbalancing narrative with systematic and theoretical analysis.

It was the great statesman Abraham Lincoln –the sitting US President when Florentine Ariosto Jones was at the age of twenty – who said, "*And in the end, it's not the years in your life that count. It's the life in your years.*" These words are a perfect fit to describe the incredible life and career of Florentine Ariosto Jones. Who was Florentine Ariosto Jones? What did he accomplish? Why do we remember him? What is his legacy? Frank Jacob explores every one of those questions in this biography. Neither a hagiography nor a panegyric, the author has succeeded in illuminating Jones's life, impact, and social context. Jacob discovers what motivated this young man from upstate New Hampshire to become a courageous entrepreneur – a businessperson who achieved great things but also had to endure the bitter taste of failure. Jones, born in Romney, New Hampshire, in 1841, experienced all of this.

From today's perspective, we see that he succeeded in setting up a transatlantic company at the age of only 27 and brought the pioneering American spirit to Switzerland. First, let us take a look at the choice of first names. "Florentine" comes from the Latin word 'Florens' for blossoming and flourishing. Ariosto refers to the poet, thinker, and humanist Ludovico Ariosto. His main work, the verse epic Orlando furioso, is considered one of the most important texts of Italian literature and was received throughout Europe. It seems that his parents sensed the will, intelligence and assertiveness that lay dormant in him. He started as a watchmaker and founded a world-renowned company in the field of fine watchmaking. His vision of combining American manufacturing technology with Swiss watchmaking expertise is still the vision kept alive to this day.

A collective of interested people and researchers formed, who intensively researched the vague idea of the history of F.A. Jones and the beginnings of IWC, tracked down new sources and better understood the connections. The latest, but perhaps not the last publication, is now provided by Frank Jacob. He devotes himself to a somewhat different angle and tells the biography of Jones from the perspective of the USA and the specific question of the global approach and the spread of the American System of Watchmaking to Switzerland. Excitement, the richness of facts, and the scientific approach will captivate the readers. I wish you a wonderful and eventful time reading this fascinating book.

Dr. David R. Seyffer
IWC Museum Curator

Introduction

A few years ago an effort was made by an over-reaching firm to introduce a cheap grade of timepieces, but the enterprise proved disastrous, and did not in the least affect either the business, or the merchantile [sic] honor of other manufacturers. As a rule, the Swiss are by far too conservative to admit of any experiment, the direct result of which they cannot count upon, and, therefore, to state that in St. Imier any more than anywhere else, there are people foolish enough to slight their work in the vain hope of increasing the profits thereof, is simply rediculous [sic] and totally at variance with facts.[1]

In March 1875, when the above quote was published, *The Jewelers Circular and Horological Review* does not leave any doubt that Swiss-produced watches seemed to be inferior to American ones, especially since the latter were industrially produced in a modern way and no longer complied with the "traditional" Swiss way of watchmaking. What is interesting is that the name of the company is not mentioned. It was the International Watch Company (IWC) in Schaffhausen, Switzerland, that this story referred to, but what is not mentioned here is the fact that it was actually founded and run by an American, Florentine Ariosto Jones (1841-1916),[2] the man the present book is about. However, Jones did not only produce watches in Switzerland between 1868 and 1876. He also introduced what David Seyffer, one of the few experts on Jones and curator of the IWC Museum in Schaffhausen, referred to as a Swiss-based American system of watchmaking.[3] This system laid the foundation for the success of the company that, regardless of some troublesome periods in the company's history, would last more than 150 years. Jones had the idea to produce high-quality watches at a low price for the American market, and

---

[1] "Swiss Watchmakers," *The Jewelers' Circular and Horological Review* 6, no. 2 (March 1875): 34.
[2] For a short biographical introduction, see "Florentine Ariosto Jones," June 30, 2015. Accessed September 15, 2019. https://www.iwc.com/de/de/articles/experiences/florentine-ariosto-jones.html.
[3] David Seyffer, "Innovation oder Nachahmung? Überlegungen zur Einführung des American System of Watch Making in der Schweiz Ende des 19. Jahrhunderts," in *Alles nur geklaut? Innovationsfähigkeit im Kontext von Technologietransfer und Industriespionage*, eds. Thomas Schuetz and David Seyffer (Stuttgart: IZKT, 2018), 9-26. Seyffer is also the author of the most detailed history of the IWC and Jones's role in that company; see David Seyffer, *Die Unternehmensgeschichte von IWC Schaffhausen: Ein Schweizer Uhrenhersteller zwischen Innovation und Tradition*, 2 vols. (Oberhausen: Athena, 2014). The references in this work all refer to vol. 1.

therefore was a pioneer with regard to the idea of exporting labor-intensive industrial production processes to cheaper foreign countries in order to sell the products to a market where the final products were not only competitive with regard to their quality but also cheaper and were therefore able both to attract buyers and, at the same time, to generate profit. He thereby was an agent of an early globalization in the watch industry, although his attempt remained a binational one that further intensified the connection between the Swiss production sites with the American market, while also applying US production processes to change the existent transatlantic watch trade. The young man's "bold decision to undertake this venture," as Hans F. Tölke and Jürgen King highlighted, "led to the fact that the only watch factory founded by an American still producing fine precision watches is situated at Schaffhausen, on the Rhine."[4]

Jones, who grew up in the northeast of the United States and learned his trade in Boston from 1856,[5] was a supposedly well-connected man of the American watch industry with a lot of insight into the industrial production processes that had been developed by the end of the American Civil War in 1865.[6] During the war, watches became so popular that Jones realized there was a chance to make money by reducing production costs with an overseas factory, which is why, as David Seyffer suitably worded it, "[t]he ideas, visions and merits of F. A. Jones can only be understood and appreciated against the background of developments taking place in watchmaking in the 19th century."[7] Jones applied the American methods of watchmaking in Switzerland and established a factory that could provide the US market with American-inspired, Swiss-made

---

[4] Hans F. Tölke and Jürgen King, *IWC: International Watch Co. Schaffhausen* (Zurich: Verlag Ineichen, 1987), 12.

[5] Dirk Rheker provides a guided tour for those interested in following Jones on the stations of his life in the 19th-century United States; see Dirk Rheker, "Auf den Spuren des Gründers," *Watch International: Das Uhrenmagazin der IWC Schaffhausen* 1 (April 2008): 27-33.

[6] Tölke and King, *IWC*, 14. For a more detailed discussion of the production of pocket watches and their role in time consciousness in the US during the 19th century, see Alexis McCrossen, "The 'Very Delicate Construction' of Pocket Watches and Time Consciousness in the Nineteenth-Century United States," *Winterthur Portfolio* 44, no. 1 (2010): 1-30. On the economic role of watch production and the "battle of the giant watchmakers" during the initial period of industrial watchmaking in the US, see Gary Hoover, "Battle of the Giant Watchmakers," *American Business History Center*, September 25, 2020. Accessed November 1, 2020. https://americanbusinesshistory.org/battle-of-the-giant-watchmakers/.

[7] David Seyffer, "Watchmaking in the 19th Century," in David Seyffer, Thomas König and Alan Myers, *F. A. Jones: His Life, Legacy and Watches* (Schaffhausen: IWC, 2013), 7.

quality watches.[8] Production methods were consequently transferred across the Atlantic, and American watchmaking was consequently exported as well as globalized because Swiss workers would produce watches according to American standards so that the result of their work could be exported and sold in the United States afterward. Jones could therefore profit from existent transatlantic logistics as they had developed since the age of exploration, turning the Atlantic into an ocean of trade[9] as well as an ocean across which knowledge and ideas, and not only those related to economic aspects of human life, were exchanged as well.[10]

Regardless of the impact Jones's attempt would have with regard to its long-term perspective, little is known about the man who brought the American system of watchmaking to Switzerland and thereby, in a way, globalized this system in the second half of the 19th century. Jones was born on 15 February 1841 in Rumney, New Hampshire, a small village first settled in the 1760s that has around 1,400 people living there today.[11] His parents, Solomon Jones (1797-1864), a shoemaker, and his wife Lavina (1800-1864), could trace their family lineage back to the time of the Pilgrim Fathers and were consequently considered to be "Mayflower

---

[8] Seyffer, *Die Unternehmensgeschichte*, 15.
[9] David Hancock, *The Sea in History: The Early Modern World* (Woodbridge: Boydell Press, 2017), 19-29; Frank Jacob and Martina Kaller, "Introduction: Commodity Trade, Globalization, and the Making of the Atlantic World," in *Transatlantic Trade and Global Cultural Transfers since 1492: More than Commodities*, eds. Martina Kaller and Frank Jacob (London/New York: Routledge, 2019), 1-12; Michael Zeuske, *Schwarze Karibik: Sklaven, Sklavereikulturen und Emanzipation* (Zurich: Rotpunktverlag, 2004).
[10] Karel Davids, *Dutch Atlantic Connections, 1680-1800: Linking Empires, Bridging Borders* (Leiden: Brill, 2014), 224-248; Wim Klooster and Gert Oostindie, *Realm between Empires: The Second Dutch Atlantic, 1680-1815* (Ithaca, NY: Cornell University Press, 2018). For a recently published and detailed study about knowledge transfer within the Atlantic world and its impact on tobacco farming, see Alexander van Wickeren, *Wissensräume im Wandel: Eine Geschichte der deutsch-französischen Tabakforschunng (1780-1870)* (Cologne: Böhlau, 2020). That not only knowledge about production and selling processes were transported across the Atlantic but also that political ideas were exchanged according to existent transatlantic networks is discussed in Frank Jacob and Mario Keßler, "Transatlantic Radicalism: A Short Introduction," in *Transatlantic Radicalism: Socialist and Anarchist Exchanges in the 19th and 20th Centuries*, eds. Frank Jacob and Mario Keßler (Liverpool: Liverpool University Press, 2021), 1-20. For the role and processes of knowledge globalization also see Pierre-Yves Donzé and Shigehiro Nishimura, eds. *Organizing Global Technology Flows: Institutions, Actors, and Processes* (London: Routledge, 2013).
[11] "A Peek at the Past... Florentine Ariosto Jones," *Rumney Historical Society*, June 20, 2018. Accessed October 1, 2019. http://rumneyhs.blogspot.com/2018/06/a-peek-at-passt-florentine-ariosto-jones.html?view=magazine.

nobility."[12] In contrast to this supposedly well-recorded family lineage, almost nothing is known about Florentine Ariosto Jones and his life, besides some facts that are frequently repeated.[13] Only his time in Switzerland is relatively well-documented, although the information at hand creates a lot of unanswered questions. As of today, for example, we do not have a clearly identified image of Jones, although the IWC uses an old photograph that supposedly shows Jones in his later years (Fig. X.1). The cover image of the present book also only shows a solider of the unit Jones served in during the Civil War, and since he is holding a watch, it was assumed that this must have been the young watchmaker in uniform. In an official record of his person, he was described in 1907 as follows: "height 5 ft. 7 1/2 ins. ..., weight 215 lbs ..., blue eyes, brown hair."[14]

Fig. X.1: Florentine Ariosto Jones, 1841-1916, IWC Archives.

---

[12] Tölke and King, *IWC*, 16.
[13] Max Ruh, "Ein Amerikaner als Schaffhauser Industriepionier," *Schaffhauser Magazin* 3 (1992): 41.
[14] Tölke and King, *IWC*, 18.

Introduction

Fig. X.2: Jones's signature, IWC Archives.

However, the lack of an actual verified photograph is not the only aspect that makes Jones's life story mysterious and intriguing. The man who found investors and lived on both sides of the Atlantic almost disappeared after his return to the United States when he turned his back on an industry that had shaped his life for so long. There is speculation about his involvement in the watch industry, as some patents are registered in his name between 1883 and 1907, but it is assumed that he worked as a salesman in the watch trade, probably in New York, before he was later employed by a company that produced steam tubes.[15] He died in Boston in 1916, yet his legacy as an American pioneer who purposefully founded the International Watch Company, according to later company advertisements,[16] in 1868 and produced watches in Switzerland for the US market was forgotten relatively soon. About the company, the same advertisement states: "This factory had to cope with all the difficulties that arise each time it is a question of introducing a completely new industry into a place which requires personnel with special knowledge."[17] In fact, the IWC and Jones had to deal with similar problems as the US watch industry at its beginning, namely an enormous need for capital investment.

One question related to this is the role of Jones during the early years of the IWC. Considering his appearance in Switzerland and disappearance in later years from the US watch industry, without any reliable sources about his whereabouts, the question comes to mind as to whether he was acting more like a con artist who just sold the people of Schaffhausen the dream of their own watch company. Such a perspectivation would probably go too far, as Jones knew how to produce watches. However, the money the American watchmaker was able to raise points to another question related to Jones's pioneering project: Was he acting alone or as part of a network of US investors he had persuaded of his ideas? Considering these aspects, there are three possible story narratives, and it must be stated here that none of them can be clearly said to be true with regard to the existing sources, which is why the final

---

[15] Ruh, "Ein Amerikaner," 41.
[16] Advertisement Catalog, Fabrique d'Horlogerie de J- Rauschenbach, n.d., IWC Archives, DM05-1151, 3.
[17] Ibid., 4.

decision must be made by each reader for herself or himself. Jones could have been

1. a con artist-like adventurer who tried to make a fortune by selling the dream of a watch company to people in Schaffhausen, who were eager to invest money to participate in what had turned out to be a global trade;
2. a single pioneer who showed guts by taking the risk in his mid-20s to move to Switzerland to build a watch company from scratch and link its production to a trade system he was well familiar with; or
3. a man chosen to represent American investors' interest in Switzerland, as they had realized that cheaper production according to the American system of watchmaking was possible; the movements produced in Switzerland were later supposed to be put together in the US and sold as American watches.

There are reasons for all of these assumptions and some are more persuasive than others.[18] I would argue that the truth might be a mix of all three, but I do not want to offer a conclusion about Jones at this point of the book. I will first present the known facts. Therefore, it is also not the aim of this book to offer a biography of Jones, as we simply know too little about the man's life, but rather to embed the facts that are known into the story of the transatlantic developments of the American system of watchmaking and its adaption in Switzerland during the second half of the 19th century. In a way, I will relate the story of a Yankee in Switzerland and how he intended to globalize American watchmaking.

In this regard, Jones was a real pioneer, whose innovative thoughts had been stimulated by his experiences within existent watch-related networks and information that was already being exchanged on a global level.[19] As Seyffer correctly emphasized, the "19th century was an age of dynamic progress across the world," a time in which "the rhythm of life was no longer determined by

---

[18] The IWC would, of course, prefer to use the second option as a narrative, especially since it offers some aspects for the marketing of watches for men in the 21st century as well. See the recent marketing campaign centered around the short film "Born of a Dream." Accessed November 1, 2020. https://www.bornofadream.com/.
[19] Seyffer, *Die Unternehmensgeschichte*, 14.

sunrise and sunset but by clocks and timetables."[20] People needed to check the time more often to coordinate their actions, be it to catch a train or to act as a military collective during the Civil War, when large armies needed to be orchestrated by their officers in more complex as well as temporally and geographically stretched battles.[21] It was obvious that time management and time discipline had become more important, and many soldiers adopted the habit of checking the actual hour during their service, thereby increasing the demand for timepieces, especially pocket watches.

The technical preconditions for the successful industrial production of watches were laid in the 1850s, yet this failed due to the lack of sufficient financial capacity. The Civil War and its impact, however, from the 1860s seemed to promise enormous sales and therefore stimulated a second wave in America's watch hysteria.[22] Industrial production would soon replace traditional manufacturing, and the watch industry was one of the key industries that emphasized this trend in the second half of the 19th century.[23] The American system of watchmaking demanded the standardization of parts, and therefore precision was needed for the production process. The implementation of such precision demanded better machines and a large sum of capital that needed to be invested to realize the mass production of high-quality watches. This necessity caused a wave of bankruptcies in the first decade of research and development, and Jones, like many of his American colleagues, would fail due to a lack of sufficient capital in

---

[20] Seyffer, "Watchmaking," 7. For a more detailed discussion of the change or rather the industrialization of time and space in the 19th century, see Wolfgang Schivelbusch, *Geschichte der Eisenbahnreise: Zur Industrialisierung von Raum und Zeit im 19. Jahrhundert*, seventh edition (Frankfurt am Main: Fischer, 2000).

[21] For a survey of military developments during the Civil War, see Brent Nosworthy, *The Bloody Crucible of Courage: Fighting Methods and Combat Experience of the Civil War* (New York: Carroll & Graf, 2003), 369-416.

[22] Seyffer, "Watchmaking," 7 and 15.

[23] For broader surveys of this process, see David A. Hounshell, *From the American System to Mass Production, 1800-1932: The Development of Manufacturing Technology in the United States* (Baltimore: Johns Hopkins University Press, 1984); Donald R. Hoke, *Ingenious Yankees: The Rise of the American System of Manufactures in the Private Sector* (New York: Columbia University Press, 1990); more concisely, see Donald Hoke, "Ingenious Yankees: The Rise of the American System of Manufactures in the Private Sector," *Business and Economic History* 14 (1985): 223-235; Jeffrey D. Sachs, *The Ages of Globalization: Geography, Technology, and Institutions* (New York: Columbia University Press, 2020), 129-168; Gerard J. Tellis and Stav Rosenzweig, *How Transformative Innovations Shaped the Rise of Nations: From Ancient Rome to Modern America* (London: Anthem Press, 2018), 213-256.

the end.[24] Regardless of this failure, Jones can not only with all sincerity be called one of the "champions of new ideas in watchmaking,"[25] but must also be seen as one of the pioneers with regard to a production process that would use transatlantic knowledge, workforce, supply chains, and sale strategies. And Jones himself emphasized the Americanness of his Swiss company, referring to it as a production site according to American standards of watchmaking.[26] It is not overemphasis when Seyffer argues that "Jones played a special if not a unique part in implementing this vision [of the American system of manufacturing] within the high-quality pocket-watch segment, which was particularly stubborn [especially in Switzerland] in its resistance to mechanized production."[27] Regardless of this resistance, however, Jones was able to establish a functioning watch company in Schaffhausen, which, despite the initial lack of capital, would turn out to become a success story. He was a champion of innovation, and this turned out to be the essential basis for this particular success story.[28]

It was in Schaffhausen that "Jones turned his dream of owning his own watch factory into reality,"[29] and his story is proof of the interrelationship between the history of technology and the business sector, i.e. the Swiss and American watch industries. Jones's story is consequently one that allows a better insight into different aspects of Swiss and US history. What started in the United States as a new system of manufacturing in the 19th century before the Civil War was taken and transplanted by Jones to Switzerland to save labor costs. The production process was consequently globalized to provide cheaper production for a market that demanded higher numbers of quality watches. Jones, who had spent many years in the American watch industry, was willing to cross the Atlantic to achieve what he could not in his home country,[30] which was to take charge of his own watch company, producing watches as cheaply as possible according to a new system of American watchmaking, and gaining both from the availability and lower price of Swiss professional labor and from a market that would supposedly be ready to buy watches from an international watch company that promised a quality that matched American models.

---

[24] Seyffer, "Innovation oder Nachahmung?" 16.
[25] Seyffer, "Watchmaking," 7.
[26] Letter by J. Rauschenbach to the City Council of Schaffhausen, October 22, 1874, City Archive Schaffhausen (Statdarchiv Schaffhausen, henceforth StdA SH), C II.58.33/001.
[27] Seyffer, "Watchmaking," 7.
[28] Seyffer, *Die Unternehmensgeschichte*, 14.
[29] Seyffer, "Watchmaking," 7.
[30] Seyffer, "Innovation oder Nachahmung?" 19.

Fig. X.3: IWC Factory Building, 1883, IWC Archive, P07–1054.

Jones, who had worked for Edward Howard in Boston, was sent to Paris to visit the second world's fair (*Exposition universelle d'art et d'industrie*) in 1867.[31] During his trip to Europe, the American watchmaker would also visit centers of Swiss watchmaking, where Jones might have developed his plan for his later venture in Schaffhausen. In the US, he had observed that there was a lack of skilled labor, which was consequently quite expensive. In Switzerland, on the other hand, there were skilled workers, but the production process was still very traditional, i.e. not industrialized yet. Jones realized that if he were able to combine the advantages of the American production system and the Swiss labor capacity, he would be able to sell many more watches than US competitors on the North American market. His idea was born, and soon after his first trip, Jones would come back to Switzerland to launch the establishment of his production site.[32]

The history of the company, which from 1869 would change its name and form quite often, shows that Jones struggled with the steady need for fresh capital. The company consequently went through the following periods, showing different legal forms and names:

---

[31] On the world fair, see the illustrated journal *L'Exposition universelle de 1867: Publication internationale autoriseée par la Commission impériale*, edited by François Ducuing, which was published to accompany the world fair.

[32] Seyffer, "Innovation oder Nachahmung?" 19-20.

1869-1871   F.A. Jones & Comp.[33]
1871-1872   F.A. Jones and International Watch Co. AG.[34]
1871-1874   International Watch Company AG/New York.[35]
1874-1876   International Watch Company, Schaffhausen.[36]

Jones was an ambitious man, considering that he wanted to sell his watches on the American market. There, US watch companies were already fighting for the highest sales, and the dismissive tone of the later report in *The Jewelers' Circular and Horological Review* cited earlier might resemble the US competitors' perspective on this bold attempt by Jones. Yet he was successful with regard to the establishment of a functioning production site, and the watches that remain from the IWC's early period prove that Jones was able to produce excellent watches.

Fig. X.4: Savonnette Pocket Watch showing a Mississippi steamship, 1874, property of Hannes A. Pantli.

All in all, and besides the things we do not know for sure about Jones, the young American was, as IWC collector and expert Thomas König worded it, "a visionary who fought all difficulties and not only designed the first quality

---

[33] Region book for the canton Schaffhausen, StdA SH, Entry No. 278.
[34] StdA SH, RRA 2/7297.
[35] IWC Archive, DC05-1000.
[36] Ibid.

watch based on the American system of watchmaking using machines, but also implemented a strategy nowadays known in the automobile industry as platform-strategy to make a broad variety of movements covering different quality levels from a few basic designs."[37] He had transferred American knowledge about industrial production procedures to Switzerland, where the new production methods would be successful, regardless of the IWC's initial failure, and therefore Jones stimulated the transition from craft to industry within the Swiss watch industry. The process initiated by the young American pioneer must, according to Seyffer, therefore be seen as the innovative basis for modern watchmaking in Switzerland.[38] The IWC acted as the "first mover,"[39] representing the idea that Swiss skilled labor combined with American technology could provide large numbers of high-quality watches for a developed industrial market.

Of course, IWC is not the only watch company that underwent major transitions in the 19th century, but the current book will focus on Jones and the early period of IWC's history to show, how early attempts were made that would later be undertaken by man Swiss watch companies.[40]

As mentioned before, the present book is an attempt to tell Jones's story while highlighting how it was embedded into the broader history of the globalization of American watchmaking. Therefore, the first chapter will provide a survey of the development of the US watch industry until and during the Civil War. Afterward, the events in Switzerland will be taken into closer consideration to discuss not only the adaptation and implementation of industrial production procedures at the IWC in Schaffhausen, but also Jones's position within this history. The book therefore offers a case study related to the biography of a bold young American in the years his actions can be reconstructed. It also offers an attempt to better understand changes in a globalizing age, namely the late 19th century, where business histories can no longer be studied or written in regional or national contexts but must be understood as global ventures. Jones's fate depended as much on successful production in Switzerland as on the sales of his watches in the United States. Whatever his role might have been in detail, with regard to his business model, Jones was a visionary and somebody who was probably way

---

[37] Thomas König, "The International Watch Company of New York, from 1872-1874," in David Seyffer, Thomas König and Alan Myers, F. A. *Jones: His Life, Legacy and Watches* (Schaffhausen: IWC, 2013), 61. Seyffer refers to Jones's concept as one of "global sourcing." Seyffer, "Innovation oder Nachahmung?" 20.
[38] Seyffer, *Die Unternehmensgeschichte*, 15.
[39] Ibid. 15 and 21.
[40] For a history of the Swiss watch industry, Pierre-Yves Donzé, *History of the Swiss Watch Industry: From Jacques David to Nicolas Hayek* (Bern: Peter Lang, 2015) is recommended.

ahead of his time. The present study ultimately offers an insight into existent transatlantic networks in the world of watches and thereby highlights how both sides of the Atlantic Ocean were dependent on each other, especially in the world of an increasingly globalized business sector like the watch industry.

1.
A Short History of American Watchmaking until the Civil War

The history of watchmaking in the United States is a very intriguing one that is based on global exchanges, research and development, and daring and failures, but also on success and quality products.[1] Initially made for practical reasons related to sea voyages and navigation, watches would become an accessoire for the masses, increasing the demands for new styles and increased accuracy. This, of course, stimulated the intensification, diversification, and accuracy of production, and the 19th century in particular would witness the impact of the watch industry as a pioneering sector for the transition of trade into industry. In the United States in particular, as Michael C. Harrold emphasized, "watchmaking was among the industries that changed America from a frontier source of natural resources to a modern supplier of technology."[2] Florentine Ariosto Jones, who had witnessed this transition through his role in the early watch producing industry, intended to take the next developmental step by increasing production even more while reducing its costs. It is therefore obvious that watches are not solely objects but artifacts that provide an insight into the history of 19th-century US history and the globalizing attempts by one of its representatives, Florentine Ariosto Jones. To better understand his thoughts and ideas, it is essential to take a closer look at the historical development of the American watch industry before this pioneer left the United States to produce watches according to the American system of watchmaking in Switzerland.[3]

---

[1] The classic study by Charles S. Crossman, *A Complete History of Watch and Clock Making in America* (New York: Jewelers' Circular Pub. Co., 1886), is still an interesting read that offers a collection of articles that were originally published in the *Jewelers' Circular and Horological Review*.

[2] Michael C. Harrold, *American Watchmaking: A Technical History of the American Watch Industry 1850-1930* (Columbia, PA: National Association of Watch and Clock Collectors, Inc., 1984), 1.

[3] Unless indicated otherwise, the following analysis is based on Harrold, *American Watchmaking*, 1-27 and Alexis McCrossen, *Marking Modern Times: A History of Clocks, Watches, and Other Timekeepers in American Life* (Chicago/London: The University of Chicago Press, 2013), 3-56.

Fig. 1.1: Marine chronometer (small longitude clock no. 1), 1777. Photo taken in the Musée des Arts et Métiers by David Monniaux, 2006.[4]

In the 1700s, English-made watches were essential for the successes of the British fleet in the Atlantic. Marine chronometers were built to support traveling and navigation across the ocean and thereby supported the expansion of the British Empire in the following centuries.

At that time, however, watches were not produced in large numbers, and there were no finished parts that could simply be used. To finish a watch would consequently take a lot of time, and the final product was not cheap for a mass market. In the 1700s, watchmaking in Europe was not exclusively an English

---

[4] Accessed May 12, 2021. https://commons.wikimedia.org/wiki/File:Berthoud_longitude_clock_p1040262.jpg.

domain, but the French and Swiss watchmakers of the time did not face similar demands from their customers to those that the British navy made of their colleagues manufacturing watches for the fleet. Considering that time management and accuracy were still the privileges of a few and not necessities for many, it is no surprise that the appearance of the watch was often more important than its functionality. Early modern timepieces of the second half of the 18th century needed to be handy and stylish to feed the needs of the fancy upper class. One demand was to construct a thinner watch, and in Paris, Jean-Antoine Lépine (1720-1814) succeeded with regard to this task when, in the 1770s, he left the full plate constructions that had been used before behind and positioned the watch's wheels under separate bridges.[5] His calibre watches were consequently thinner and made new case designs and better usability for pocket watches possible.

Fig. 1.2: Portrait of Jean-Antoine Lépine.[6]

---

[5] Lépine's watches were quite famous, and US President George Washington (1732-1799) even possessed one of them. Beson J. Lossing, *Mount Vernon and Its Associations: Historical, Biographical, and Pictoral* (New York: Townsend, 1859), 207. On Lépine's life and work, see Adolphe Chapiro, *Jean-Antoine Lépine, horloger (1720-1814): Histoire du développement de l'horlogerie en France, de 1760 à l'Empire* (Paris: Editions de l'amatuer, 1988).

[6] Accessed May 12, 2021. https://commons.wikimedia.org/wiki/File:Jean-Antoine_L%C3%A9pine.jpg.

While significant developments had been made in Europe, the North American colonies were initially more important as export markets for watches from England, France, and Switzerland. Regardless of the fact that English fabricates had dominated this market for quite some time, better watches were soon to be imported from Switzerland and would eventually also be produced in the United States, where the watch business became particularly important in the 19th century. New technological assets were applied too late by the English watch manufacturers, who fell behind their competitors. Colonial America was hardly a threat to the imperial center and its watch production facilities, but the independent nation state would prove more than capable of causing problems for the spoiled English producers.

Fig. 1.3: Illustration of a Goddard watch from 1812, Pocket Watch Database.[7]

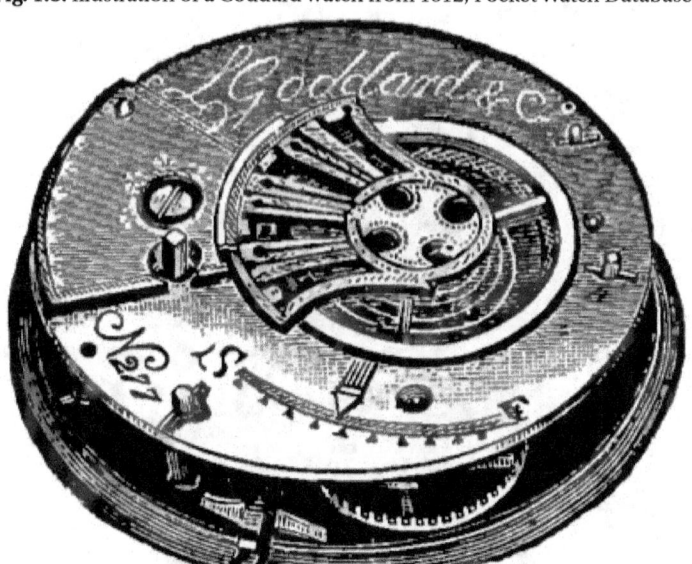

THE GODDARD WATCH.

Nevertheless, the first American watchmakers were often immigrants who had begun to provide local services for the repair of imports before the first attempts were made to establish a genuinely American production system for watches. Hence, regardless of these long-term developments, the first American watchmakers, like Luther Goddard (1762-1842) of Shrewsbury,

---

[7] Accessed May 12, 2021. https://pocketwatchdatabase.com/assets/images/history/goddard-watch-movement.jpg.

Massachusetts, had to rely on the same methods to assemble the movements and the watches as a whole that had been used by their English colleagues during the late 18th and early 19th centuries.[8]

Although watchmakers like Goddard were able to manufacture quality watches, they were unable to produce them in significant numbers and consequently only sold relatively few on the American market, at least when one compares the numbers to watches imported from Europe, mainly from England and Switzerland. The value of imported watches increased year on year, and it was not surprising that American manufacturers eventually wanted to gain influence and their personal share from the growing demands for timepieces. US President Thomas Jefferson's (1743-1826) Embargo Act of 1807 decreased the number of imports in the years of the Napoleonic Wars (1803-1815) and stimulated ways to replace European goods, although it also urged people to smuggle trading goods that were demanded by American consumers.[9]

The embargo did not last long, however, and the English-American relationships within the transatlantic watch trade continued. However, there was a change with regard to some aspects, as American watchmakers began to import parts from England that they would assemble on their own and sell the final product as an American-made watch. Luther Goddard tried this in the 1810s after the embargo, but he could only produce a few hundred watches before 1817, when production stopped again. Goddard simply could not offer competitive prices, especially with regard to the watches imported from Switzerland, and therefore had to give up his idea of his own American watch production.

However, one can trace a continuity from Goddard's early attempts to the more successful ventures of the following decades. His apprentices, Jubal Howe and William Keith, continued to work according to their predecessor's ideas. Both of them would later use their skills to play a role in Boston, where the first modern watch companies, like the Boston Watch Company and the American Watch Company, would be established. The industrialization of American watchmaking in particular highlights the role of individual knowledge for successful industrialization and production, as skills came in with people who could be persuaded to join the new factories and thereby invest their know-how in a new environment as well as in the success of their new employers. And Goddard was not the only one who had experimented with watch production.

---

[8] Henry G. Abbott, *The Watch Factories of America: Past and Present* (Chicago: Geo. K. Hazlitt & Co., 1888), 15.

[9] Lawrence S. Kaplan, "Jefferson, the Napoleonic Wars, and the Balance of Power," *William and Mary Quarterly* 14, no. 2 (1957): 196-217; John Meacham, *Thomas Jefferson: The Art of Power* (New York: Random House, 2013), 425-435; Harvey Strum, "Rhode Island and the Embargo of 1807," *Rhode Island History* 52, no 2 (1994): 58-67.

Jacob Custer (1810-1879) had also produced watches with an individual design in Norristown, Pennsylvania in the early 1840s. Although they had still applied traditional methods to produce watches as individual pieces, they stimulated interest in American watches by offering the possibility to buy such products in the first half of the 19th century. Later, nevertheless, watchmakers would apply new production methods, but these were not invented in the watch business at first.

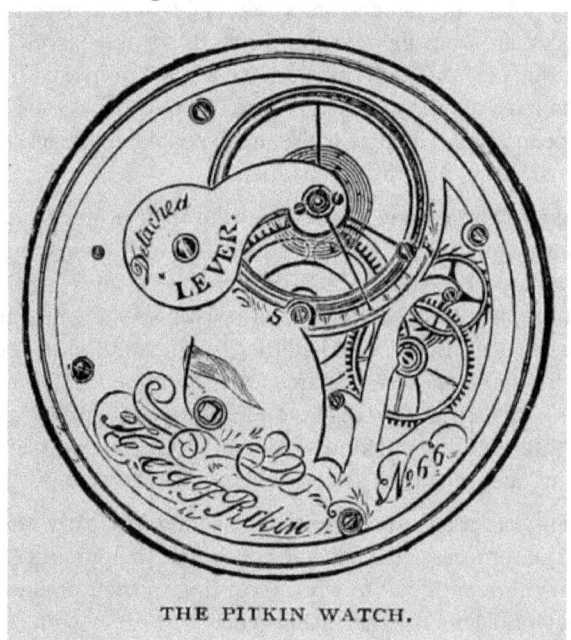

Fig. 1.4: The Pitkin watch, 1838.[10]

Eli Terry (1772-1852) was an American inventor in Connecticut who had begun to use machines to produce higher numbers of parts, especially for the production of wooden clock parts, that soon reached an output one could not have imagined before.[11] Others experimented with similar ideas, especially with regard to the production of rifles for the US military. In both production branches, people experimented with interchangeable parts to allow for larger

---

[10] PD-US. Accessed May 12, 2021. https://commons.wikimedia.org/wiki/File:Pitkin_Watch_c_1838.png.

[11] Kenneth D. Roberts and Snowden Taylor, *Eli Terry and the Connecticut Shelf Clock*, second edition (Fitzwilliam, NH: Ken Roberts Publishing Company, 1994). See also Diana Muir, *Reflections in Bullough's Pond: Economy and Ecosystem in New England* (Hanover, NH: University of New England Press, 2000), 119-135.

quantities to be produced in a shorter amount of time. The origin of the modern watch industry of the United States was in Hartford, Connecticut, where the Pitkin brothers, Henry (1811-1846) and James (1812-1870), experimented with new production methods and in 1838 presented the so-called Pitkin watch.

However, as Henry G. Abbott remarked in 1888, "[t]he Pitkin watch, however, dared the same fate as its predecessors. The cost of manufacture was too great to compete with those made by the Swiss, and shortly after moving the factory to New York, which they did in 1841, the idea was abandoned. The total product of the Pitkins was about 800 movements."[12] Soon after their move to New York, the Pitkins' company closed because they could not secure sufficient profits from their watches. Jones would face the same problem in Switzerland, as the transformation to an industrial production system was very cost-intensive, and many of the early pioneers simply lacked the capital to survive long enough until profits could actually be created by an enormous output and subsequent sales. However, the Pitkins would not be the last who experimented with the interchangeability of parts, and others—including inventors in Switzerland, e.g. the watchmaker Pierre-Frédéric Ingold (1787-1878),[13] England, and France—would continue the quest to reach a production process that would be based on this principle. Regardless of these international approaches in the early 1800s, it would be American inventors who fully embraced the idea to completely transform production methods to achieve an industrialized system of watchmaking. They "turned philosophy into large scale action, developing an industry that changed watchmaking the world over."[14]

Hence the industry needed time to reach its full functionality and productivity. And naturally, its final achievements must be considered the result of a long process of research and development[15] as well as of changing perceptions of time, causing stricter time management and increasing the demand for more watches. In addition, the process as such was not solely dominated by watchmakers but also by jewelers, who were active in producing and selling watches throughout the United States as well. They had monopolized their own

---

[12] Abbott, *The Watch Factories of America*, 16.
[13] Georges-Albert Berner and Emil Audétat, *Schweizer Pioniere der Wirtschaft und Technik*, vol 13 (Zurich: Verein für Wirtschaftshistorische Studien, 1962); Jules-Frederick-Urban Jürgensen, *De l'emploi des machines en horlogerie: Spécialement dans la fabrication des montres de poche* (Neuchâtel: Wolfrath et Metzner, 1877).
[14] Harrold, *American Watchmaking*, 15.
[15] Chris H. Bailey, *Two Hundred Years of American Clocks and Watches* (Englewood Cliffs, NJ: Prentice-Hall, 1975); George H. Eckhardt, *United States Clock and Watch Patents, 1790-1890: The Record of a Century of American Horology and Enterprise* (New York: n.p., 1960).

position within the watch trade since its beginning in the 17th century, and all kinds of clocks and watches—from new to used and in different forms and designs—would have to go through their hands. It was the jewelers who, as investors, would stimulate the industrialization process within the watch business because they often provided the necessary capital due to their interest to sell larger numbers of watches to a growing market of customers across the whole country. Yet the jewelers were not just important economically; they also provided local time control through special astronomical knowledge and respective instruments for larger groups of local people. With regard to this time regime and the introduction of standard times, watchmakers and jewelers also participated in a nation state-building process by helping to centralize local times according to the new national centers, and the standard time was determined by the latter for the whole country. They thereby secured control and political power in the political center over the still often rural periphery.[16]

Initially, time did not offer a mass-oriented business, but larger tower clocks would become relevant timepieces in a growing number of communities.[17] Edward Howard (1813-1904) and his company in Boston, which would also play an important role in US pocket watch production, and Seth Thomas (1785-1859), with his factory in Connecticut, were the main producers and sold many of the around 5,000 public clocks—2,036 non-striking and 3,118 striking ones—that were installed between 1871 and 1911. By the end of the 19th century, it was not only the possession of pocket watches but also the installment of public clocks that had reached a peak in the United States.[18]

Table 1.1: Clock types and numbers sold by Edward Howard's and Seth Thomas's companies between 1871 and 1911.[19]

Clock Type	Striking	Non-Striking	Percentage of all sales
Tower	957	657	51%
Interior clock	28	842	28%
Post	1	251	8%
Façade	82	108	6%

---

[16] McCrossen, *Marking Modern Times*, 4.
[17] For a detailed survey, see Frederick Shelley, *Early American Tower Clocks: Surviving American Tower Clocks from 1726-1870* (Columbia, PA: National Association of Watch and Clock Collectors, 1999).
[18] McCrossen, *Marking Modern Times*, 6-7.
[19] Ibid., 7.

The popularity of public clocks during the 19th century increased similarly to that of pocket watches. The existence of the two different timepieces went hand in hand, as many customers might have been inspired to buy individual pocket watches by the existent of a visible display of a central timepiece, according to which one could schedule one's own life and its time. Alexis McCrossen highlights in this regard that "[t]he near mania for public timepieces in the United States coincided with a vogue for towers, monuments, and monumental forms."[20] The forging of an imagined community[21] was in a way not only made possible by modern print capitalism but similarly by a shared time regime, which was based on the acceptance of being part of a particular and centrally determined time zone. With technological innovations, timepieces, be they tower clocks or pocket watches, became cheaper and more widely distributed, and were thereby similarly responsible for the creation of a national time regime.

In contrast to former reliances on natural phenomena, like the sun or the moon, to count hours or months, people now relied on their own mastery of time and the technologies that had been provided to do so. Local standards and local time regimes demanded more and more clocks, and these necessities and the changing human relationship with time thereby paved the way for the technological innovations of the 19th century. Simply speaking, to quote McCrossen again, "[w]atches made time portable"[22] and helped to spread national standards, like a centralized time, step by step across the whole nation state, where formerly rural and peripheral regions developed to act according to the national pulse of time. It was especially the new railroads and their use by ordinary people to travel that also stimulated the spread of the above-mentioned time regime. At the same time, this particular aspect of transportation—crossing the continent from coast to coast from 1869—made more accurate time-keeping and consequently more precise watches necessary.[23] In addition, "ever closer

---

[20] Ibid., 8.

[21] Benedict Anderson, *Imagined Communities. Reflections on the Origin and Spread of Nationalism* (London: Verso, 1983).

[22] McCrossen, *Marking Modern Times*, 13.

[23] On the impact of the railroads in the American South see, among other works, the introduction provided in "Railroad Industry," in *The New Encyclopedia of Southern Culture, vol. 11: Agriculture and Industry*, ed. John F. Stover (Chapel Hill, NC: University of North Carolina Press, 2008), 317-319. See also Peter A. Hansen, "Still Controversial: The Pacific Railroad at 150," *Railroad History* 208 (2013): 8-35. On railroad watches, see Adriano Davidoni, "A Short History of Railroad Watches," *Watch Time Middle East*, March 10, 2017. Accessed November 1, 2020. https://watchtime.me/life-style/vintage/article/832/a-short-history-of-railroad-watches.

attention to coordination, synchronization, and precision in time-keeping"[24] was demanded, and consequently watchmakers were also confronted by these wishes from their potential customers. The developments in the American watch industry during the 19th century were therefore related to different overlapping interests, as they were being expressed not only by the producers of different watches but also by customers, scientists, politicians, and everyone else who had an interest in a more precise and widespread form of time management.

Fig. 1.5: Photograph of the ceremony for the completion of the First Transcontinental Railroad and the driving of the golden spike at Promontory Summit, Utah, May 10, 1869. Samuel S. Montague of the Central Pacific Railroad and Grenville M. Dodge of the Union Pacific Railroad shake hands.[25]

With the growing availability of steadily more precise watches, time "conquered" ever-increasing parts of American life, and both public clocks and personal ones, mostly pocket watches, determined the modern time regime in all parts of the country. Different watch models and types could be found throughout the United States, and more and more places, e.g. factories, offices,

---

[24] McCrossen, *Marking Modern Times*, 15.
[25] PD-US. Accessed May 12, 2021. https://commons.wikimedia.org/wiki/File:East_and_West _Shaking_hands_at_the_laying_of_last_rail_Union_Pacific_Railroad.jpg?uselang=de

train stations, etc., displayed the time by the installment of public clocks. "In the 1880s and 1890s, time-recording clocks, timecard systems, and automatic time stamps were introduced; by the 1900s, the International Time Recording Company, which would become International Business Machines (IBM) had consolidated the industry."[26] Clocks and watches had consequently "naturalized the hegemonic use of hours and minutes to measure time,"[27] and due to this development, more and more people sensed the need to get their own timepieces to become part of American modernity as well.

The story of the American watch industry, which lasted until the middle of the 20th century—when many companies had already moved their production sites to Switzerland[28]—and the famous Elgin National Watch Company went out of business in 1960, began as a success in the second half of the 19th century, an "epoch when American uses of and dreams about bells, clocks, time balls, standard time, and pocket watches together made and marked modern time."[29] Although the number of clocks and watches had already increased during the 18th century, it had not been a commodity made for mass consumption or mass use, to be more precise. They were, and even remained in later times, a status symbol that could display their owners' financial capacities, and during the 19th century all kinds of watches were sold due to this social function of the watch as well. In the late 18th century, however, the Willard brothers in Grafton, Massachusetts had introduced a cheap wooden alternative that could be inexpensively purchased, and as mentioned before, Eli Terry was one who experimented with the mass production of such wooden watch parts some years later. Of course, watch importers and jewelers, who sold these imports, initially aimed for upper-class customers, but due to the economic developments of the 19th century, the mid-price segment became more and more important, especially since watch production became much cheaper as well. The so-called "Banjo clocks" of the Willard brothers, with their wooden parts and affordable prices, soon hung or stood in many American homes.

---

[26] McCrossen, *Marking Modern Times*, 20.
[27] Ibid., 23.
[28] One of these transatlantic moves was made by *Bulova Watches*. Aaron Sigmond, *Bulova: A History of Firsts* (New York: Assouline Publishing, 2017).
[29] McCrossen, *Marking Modern Times*, 23.

Fig. 1.6: A Banjo clock created by Aaron Willard, 1815-1825, Metropolitan Museum of Art, New York, NY.[30]

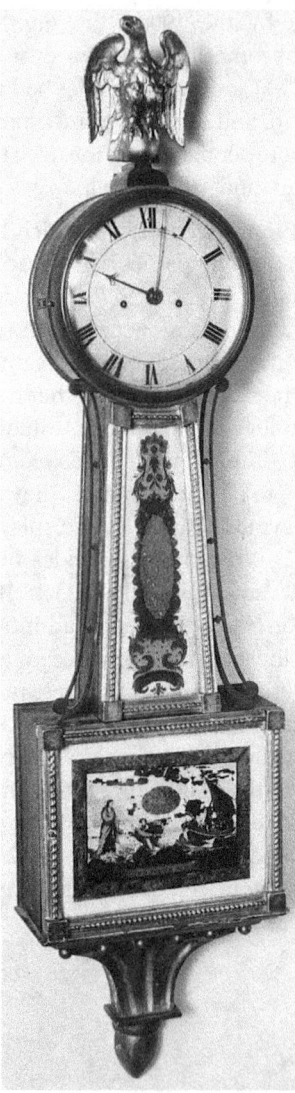

It was the success of the Willard brothers with their higher numbers of sales that stimulated further interest in the production of clocks and watches, and that allowed the above-mentioned Eli Terry to begin his experiments with regard to the mass production of parts for a growing number of customers, who

---

[30] PD-US. Accessed May 12, 2021. https://www.metmuseum.org/art/collection/search/317.

would eventually sell the assembled clocks. Next to clocks, the demand for watches also increased during the early decades of the 19th century, and watchmaker Frederick Reed advertised in *Paxton's Philadelphia Advertiser* (1818) that he had "constantly on hand a general assortment of Gold and Silver Patent Lever and Plain Watches, which he will dispose of on the most reasonable terms, by whole sale or retail." Jehu Ward, another advertiser, highlighted that he had "constantly on hand a general assortment of Double and Single cased warranted Watches, Chains, Seals, Keys, Silver Table and Tea Spoons, Sugar Tongs, &c. ... offer[ed], wholesale or retail at reduced prices."[31] Combined with a growing number of church bells[32] and public clocks, the pocket watch turned out to be one of the manufactured goods that was most demanded by an increasing number of customers, who also wanted to keep time control in their own hands.[33]

Another technology that was important for centralized time from the early 1840s—as well as for the control and expansion of imperial control in other parts of the world—was the telegraph.[34] It made the distribution and control of standard times much easier, and in Great Britain, a national standard time was introduced in 1848, setting the mark for other countries to follow that policy. One year later, a standard time was introduced in New England, with Boston as the point of reference. Wishes to follow a standard time were expressed more often once the telegraph had provided the possibility for its steady control. Thanks to astronomer and clockmaker William C. Bond (1789-1859),[35] signals would be available directly from the Harvard College Observatory, which allowed the provision of very accurate time information via telegraph lines. Soon afterward, other local observatories would offer the same service, and the respective authorities responsible for public clocks could check and apply the exact time, which would then be adopted by those who owned a pocket watch or clock at home.

---

[31] Both advertisements are reproduced in McCrossen, *Marking Modern Times*, 37.
[32] Some famous production sites and their output shall be named here: the Meneely Bell Company in upstate New York produced 65,000 bells, the Verdin Company in Ohio produced 50,000 bells from 1840, and the McShane Bell Foundry, originally operating in Baltimore, MD, produced 300,000 bells from 1856. Ibid., 45.
[33] Charlene E. Stephens, *On Time: How America Has Learned to Live by the Clock* (Boston: Bulfinch Press Book, 2002), especially the chapters "Telling time 1700-1820" and "Mechanizing time 1820-1880."
[34] Roland Wenzlhuemer, Connecting the Nineteenth-Century World: The Telegraph and Globalization (Cambridge: Cambridge University Press, 2012).
[35] "History," *Harvard College Observatory*. Accessed November 2, 2020. https://hco.cfa.harvard.edu/history.

Fig. 1.7: William C. Bond.[36]

That the existence of different time standards could be confusing can be shown by a look at New York in the early to mid-1800s, where prominent watch importer Samuel Hammond, the jeweler Samuel Benedict, as well as the Atlas clock at the front of Tiffany's & Co. were among those providing one of six possible standard times for the city. The same could be said for other regions and cities of the United States, where people struggled with different times that made its regulation difficult. The example of New York, however, shows that the existence of watches alone did not solve the problems related to time completely; a uniform time standard was needed as well, and the latter could only be provided by the necessary technological advances in combination with the affordability of precise timepieces. Both of these issues, however, would be tackled in the following years.

---

[36] PD-US. Accessed May 12, 2021. https://commons.wikimedia.org/wiki/File:PSM_V47_D300_William_Cranch_Bond.jpg.

Fig. 1.8: Atlas with the clock at the Tiffany & Company Building, 727 Fifth Avenue, New York. Courtesy of Tristan Surtel, photo taken by Meg Lessard, June 8, 2014.[37]

Cheaper clocks and watches, like the wooden ones mentioned before with regard to the early production in Connecticut, were provided by peddlers who sold those as well as cheap imports in all parts of the United States. European watches became more and more readily available, acting as artifacts that prove the existence of intensive transatlantic trade relationships between European producers on the one hand and US customers on the other. At the same time, however, the market share of American-made clocks and watches increased. In

---

[37] Accessed May 12, 2021. https://commons.wikimedia.org/wiki/File:Clock_Tiffany_%26_Company_Building.jpg.

Connecticut, Chauncey Jerome (1793-1868), to name just one example, produced more than 250,000 brass clocks per year in his two factories there during the 1840s, and he was able to sell them as cheap as $1.50 per clock.[38] Considering the growing demand for watches, it is also not surprising that Swiss watchmakers, including the traditional company Patek Philippe, sent representatives to the United States in the 1850s to intensify existent trade relationships as well as to forge new ones with jewelers and wholesale traders who could sell their products on the other side of the Atlantic.

Fig. 1.9: A clock from Chauncey Jerome's clock company (according to markings inside), presumed 19th century. Photo taken by JVGJ, personal acquaintance of User: Bunchofgrapes, May 31, 2016.[39]

---

[38] McCrossen, *Marking Modern Times*, 56.
[39] Accessed May 12, 2021. https://de.m.wikipedia.org/wiki/Datei:Chauncey_Jerome_Clock.jpg.

With the growth of the US market and demands for second-hand watches, one would assume that prices were high, but the increased competition in this market from American manufacturers led to a price drop for the segment of foreign imports that made the above-mentioned deals between foreign producers and US sellers necessary. One could buy English watches for $30 a piece, while Swiss watches were priced as low as $15. It should be noted, however, that at that time, the daily income of an American worker was less than one dollar per day—i.e. ten working hours. The watches consequently remained something that could not easily be afforded by everyone, yet a lot of people desired to possess one. The economic developments in the first half of the 19th century had in addition created a new middle class, whose members expressed their new status through the display of expensive consumer goods, which also means watches that were worn on chains with decorative chatelains to emphasize status. What can also be observed is the availability of watches for different price ranges. While European watchmakers continued to produce high-priced watches for a limited market, from the mid-19th century, American watchmakers tried to produce cheaper watches to cover a broader market and to increase their income. It took one and a half decades to finally reach the level of mass production for which the American system of watchmaking was designed, but the long process of research and development proves that the ideas and dreams of those who worked for this process were tremendously important to the technological advances.

There were three categories of watches that were produced in the United States in the second half of the 19th century, namely 1) jeweled watches in a higher price segment, 2) inexpensive jeweled watches for the growing middle class, and 3) dollar watches for all others who could not afford more expensive watches. The availability of watches in the latter two categories shows that watches had, in contrast to the early 19th century, turned into a more common mass good. Those producers who became interested in selling higher numbers of cheap watches to a mass-market experimented with new production methods, while the higher-priced jeweled watches initially continued to secure their income. Michael C. Harrold remarks with regard to the diversification of the market that "[i]n fact, companies specializing in inexpensive jeweled watches did not appear till 1883, later than the dollar watch. Even then such factories lived a compromised existence for they made neither the best nor the cheapest watches. Therefore only a few companies succeeded … as a fulltime business."[40] The dollar watches that became available in the late 1870s were eventually the proof that the production of watches for almost everyone was possible, and although they were cheap, they worked quite well.

---

[40] Harrold, *American Watchmaking*, 3.

Between 1850 and 1930, the development of the watch industry can be divided into the following periods: 1) 1850-1860 Development, 2) 1860-1880 Expansion, 3) 1880-1910 Competition, and 4) 1910-1930 Decline.[41] In the first two, the American system of watchmaking was characterized by a strict division of labor with regard to the production of watch parts that had been standardized and produced in large numbers, the use of machines to produce parts, and a central place for production.[42] The first period between 1850 and 1860 was determined by the efforts of some pioneers in watchmaking, who experimented with new methods of mechanized parts production. This initial phase of research and development, however, showed that enormous amounts of capital were needed to achieve the pioneers' ambitious aims, and the first companies consequently went bankrupt. The second period of expansion was stimulated by the Civil War and a growing demand for watches that eventually caused new companies to be founded in 1864. This trend continued in the years until 1880, and this period saw the founding of the IWC in Switzerland, where Jones tried to replicate the American development with cheaper Swiss labor. However, growing competition within the watch market and an economic recession in the 1870s caused many problems for some of the companies, including Jones's Swiss one.

While the number of watches in circulation was still relatively low in the 1850s, their numbers steadily increased, and there was a boom in the 1860s, very much impacted by the Civil War, due to which many men would see the watch as a practical and social accessory. The watch would eventually become a mass phenomenon, and unlimited sales numbers would promise enormous gains if one could satisfy the need for cheaper quality watches.

According to Harrold, "[t]he founder of the American watch industry was Aaron Lufkin Dennison [1812-1895]. ... [He] was an inventive mechanic, adventurous businessman, apostle of the industrial revolution, and salesman of contagious enthusiasm."[43] He had moved to Boston in 1833 to learn more about watch production and repairing, and he worked for Jones, Lows & Ball together with Jubal Howe, a talented watchmaker. In 1839 he had established his own business for watch tools and had by then also developed what is known as Dennison

---

[41] Ibid. In contrast to Harrold, Seyffer names three periods between 1849 and 1910: 1) 1849-1857 Learning and experimentation, 2) 1858-1870 Specification and standardization of parts, and 3) 1871-1910 Automatization of the production and organization of production sites. Seyffer, "Innovation oder Nachahmung?" 18.
[42] Ibid.
[43] Harrold, *American Watchmaking*, 16.

Standard Gauge, a tool that was used for the measuring of mainsprings.[44] His business worked well, and in the 1840s he hired Nelson P. Stratton, a talented watchmaker who had previously worked for the Pitkin brothers as well as the Springfield Armory. At the same time, Dennison began to seriously think about the possibilities of producing watches by using machines for the preparation of interchangeable parts.[45] He therefore laid the foundations for the developments that would follow, and he would also have an impact on the young Jones, who would be inspired by Dennison's idea and intrigued by his spirit as an innovative businessman.

Fig. 1.10: Aaron Lufkin Dennison. Portrait from Abbott's *The Watch Factories of America* (1888).

Dennison, who had observed the production process in the Springfield Armory, thought about the possibilities of applying similar methods for watch

---

[44] Ibid.
[45] On his life, work, and legacy, see Philip T. Priestley, *Aaron Lufkin Dennison: An Industrial Pioneer and His Legacy* (Columbia, PA: National Association of Watch and Clock Collectors, 2009).

production, and since he "was the sort who turned ideas into action,"[46] he would try to set up a new company to do so. He approached Edward Howard with his idea, and they agreed to work together to industrialize watch production in the United States to feed an increasing market.[47] In the late 1840s, the two men undertook the first serious approach to turn trade into industry by applying modern machines for the production process. They went through numerous years of research and development as well as trials and errors before they were eventually able to establish what would later be turned into the Waltham Watch Company, one of the most influential watch companies in US history.[48]

In 1850, Dennison and Howard, together with David Davis from Roxbury, Massachusetts, founded the American Horologe Company, and Dennison went on a journey to England to find out more about the production processes there. It is consequently more than obvious that this venture imported knowledge from the other side of the Atlantic to further improve its own watches.[49] Dennison also seems to have brought some English and Swiss watchmakers back with him, and thereby also "imported" skills and know-how for his American company.[50] Howard, "[a]s a businessman … proved to be clever as well as ambitious."[51] He wanted to invest in the new company, as he considered it a way to make enormous gains if the methods Dennison had been thinking about could really be applied. Next to Howard, Samuel Curtis—Dennison's father-in-law—was an important investor, who provided $80,000 over the next few years.

While Dennison was in England gathering information, Howard would set up a suitable production site in Roxbury. Once Dennison had returned, he began experimenting with designs and machines, but the first attempts were rather unsuccessful. Eventually, as Harrold emphasized, "Dennison turned out to excel more in the overall task of superintendent than as hardware designer."[52] Nevertheless, he had realized this as well and had no problem in hiring people who would be able to solve the problems he could not. Dennison therefore

---

[46] Harrold, *American Watchmaking*, 17.
[47] Seyffer, "Watchmaking," 17.
[48] Charles W. Moore, *Timing a Century: History of the Waltham Watch Company* (Cambridge, MA: Harvard University Press, 2014 [1945]). See also Seyffer, "Innovation oder Nachahmung?" 17.
[49] Similar processes can be observed with other national watch industries as well. Pierre-Yves Donzé, *Industrial Development, Technology Transfer, and Global Competition: A History of the Japanese Watch Industry since 1850* (London: Routledge, 2017).
[50] Seyffer, "Watchmaking," 17.
[51] Harrold, *American Watchmaking*, 17.
[52] Ibid.

hired Charles Moseley to work on the production process and John Lynch, who was supposed to take care of the jeweling. It is essential to highlight that Dennison thereby tried to centralize knowledge from different parts of New England to work in the factory in Roxbury. But there were numerous problems, including difficulties related to dial making. Due to these problems, John Gold was sent to England again to gather information. He was supposed to gain insights into relevant practices in Liverpool. However, this was not the only information that had to be gathered in England. When the first watches were close to completion, there were issues with the gilding of the plate finish. As a result of this issue, Nelson Stratton learned about English gilding methods in Coventry through some early form of industrial espionage. Again, it was clear that industrial watchmaking was the result of transatlantic knowledge acquisition or exchanges. This also means that the American system of watchmaking had, in a sense, already been globalized before Jones took it to Switzerland in the late 1860s.

In 1851, the American Horologe Company was finally able to offer its first pocket watch that was built on a full plate and ran with a 30-hour power reserve.[53] Although they struggled, this American success would inspire the ambitions of other inventors and investors. At the same time, Dennison and his fellows continued to extend their design series and to produce more output. A year later, they presented 17 different models for eight-day watches, whose prototypes had been designed and constructed by the Marsh brothers, to a group of possible investors. Another year later, in 1853, the first 100 of Howard, Davis & Dennison's 30-hour watches went onto the market. By then, the company was named the Boston Watch Company, and since 1853 numerous watches have been sold under this brand name. Soon, the production site was no longer large enough to match the demand, so Dennison purchased more land in Waltham, Massachusetts along the Charles River. In October 1854, the company had 100 workers, although initially they had only produced 6-10 watches. The output could probably have been increased in the near future, but when a general recession hit the country in 1856, the watch company was in particular trouble. Although Dennison was able to bring in new investors like the New York wholesaler Fellows & Schell, when sales dropped in late 1856, the costs of production could no longer be paid. Eventually, the Boston Watch Company went bankrupt and was sold at an auction in April 1857. The New York wholesaler Royal Robbins bought it for $56,000 and were happy about their success in buying it, as they believed that the company could make a lot of money once the general recession had passed.

---

[53] Seyffer, "Watchmaking," 17.

Fig. 1.11: Waltham Factory, Boston Watch Company.[54]

There were other bidders as well who had an interest in buying the watch company, especially since "Dennison and Howard had succeeded technically, even if they fizzled financially. The American watch was being accepted by both the jewelry trade and the buying public."[55] Royal Robbins reorganized the Boston Watch Company as Appleton, Tracy, & Co., while Dennison left. The Waltham model 57 was a kind of hybrid of watchmaking, bringing together some features of English watches with some genuine American elements. However, with a price of $40 per watch, it was still not really competitive with regard to the prices of imported pocket watches.

Soon after the end of the Boston Watch Company, American-made watches became more popular, and their lower prices made them affordable for more possible buyers. Swiss manufacturers also recognized this trend and therefore began to copy styles and sizes. In 1859, the company name of Appleton, Tracy, & Co. was changed to the American Watch Co. and again in 1885 to the Waltham Watch Co., which would remain its name until the end of the famous American company, whose management continued to belong to Royal E. Robbins (1824-

---

[54] PD-US. Accessed May 12, 2021. https://commons.wikimedia.org/wiki/File:WalthamWatchCompany.jpg.

[55] Harrold, *American Watchmaking*, 21.

1902), who had "emerged in 1859 with control over 85 percent of the Boston Watch Company, whose name changed to the American Watch Company. Robbins understood that 'Americanness' enhanced the value of his company's timepieces; there was a growing market for *American* watches."[56]

Fig. 1.12: Movement of a Waltham model 57, photo taken by Bonsairolex, September 10, 2011.[57]

Dennison nevertheless continued his life as an inventor and argued for methods to produce even cheaper models. Edward Howard, in the meantime, would manage the oldest production site in Roxbury, where he continued to produce watches. Fifteen men followed him from the Waltham Watch Company. The watches produced by the old Boston Watch Company were sold under the name of Howard & Rice, the latter referring to Charles Rice, an investor who had supported Howard financially. It took Howard some years to pay his creditors back, but in the end, he and his nephew, Albert Howard, eventually produced

---

[56] McCrossen, *Marking Modern Times*, 59.
[57] Accessed December 18, 2020. https://commons.wikimedia.org/wiki/File:Waltham_model_57_movement_photo.jpg. Other images of early Waltham watches can be found in the Pocket Watch Database. Accessed December 18, 2020. https://pocketwatchdatabase.com/guide/company/waltham/images?filterSize=18&filterJewels=all&filterMovementSetting=all&filterModels=1857.

watches under the name E. Howard & Company. The Howard watches were of good quality, and the pioneer of American watchmaking, as Harrold remarked, "never sacrificed quality to achieve quantity, so that the total production after more than 40 years was barely above 100,000 watches. His efforts established a reputation for building superior watches commanding superior prices. This maintained a strong company till 1903 when it was sold to the Keystone Watchcase Company, who introduced new high-grade models bearing the name E. Howard Co."[58] Howard's watches were consequently not produced for mainstream customers. Other producers, however, would eventually fully turn the pocket watch into a mass product of American consumer culture.

The Boston Watch Company was not the only company that went bankrupt in the initial period of research and development that was necessary to establish and implement the American system of watchmaking. The short-lived Nashua Watch Co. is another example.[59] There the inventors tried to go even further than Howard, who still considered some kind of handmade finishing to be an essential aspect for American-made watches. The Nashua group wanted to produce fully industrially but struggled with the financial necessities to fulfill this plan. Nevertheless, the story of Belding Dart Bingham, the founder of the Nashua Watch Co., who had worked for the Waltham Watch Company before, shows quite well that there was a specific group of people that shared their knowledge due to their experiences in the early period of American watchmaking. It is therefore not surprising that the Nashua Watch Co. was bought by Waltham again after its bankruptcy.

The combination of the knowledge and expertise of the two companies would eventually also be visible during the Philadelphia Centennial Exposition in 1876, when the Waltham Watch Co. presented the results of precise industrialized watchmaking that would shock Swiss watchmakers. The early companies had developed special movements, which set the standards for US watches in the years to come, namely Waltham's English-style full plate, Nashua's English-style 3/4-plate, and Howard's split-plate design. The "fundamental advantage of easy assembly"[60] would make the American production process much cheaper, and the Swiss watchmaking industry would therefore suffer a bitter blow in the late 19th century.

---

[58] Harrold, *American Watchmaking*, 21.
[59] Thomas De Fazio, "The Nashua Venture and The American Watch Company," *Bulletin of the National Association of Watch and Clock Collectors, Inc.* 17, no. 6 (1975): 574-589.
[60] Harrold, *American Watchmaking*, 25.

Fig. 1.13: E. Howard & Co. Watch Advertisement, 1930.[61]

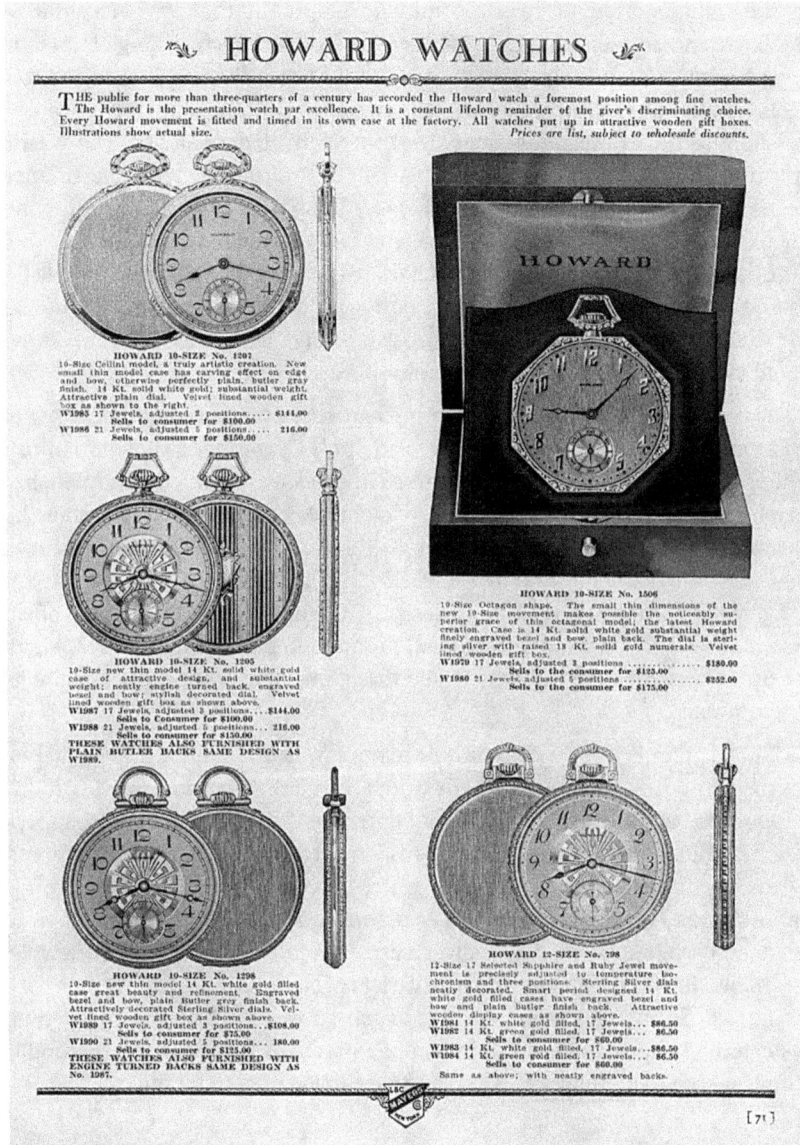

---

[61] US-PD. Accessed May 12, 2021. http://www.old-pocketwatches.com/edward-howard-pocket-watch/.

The Boston Watch Company was not the only company that went bankrupt in the initial period of research and development that was necessary to establish and implement the American system of watchmaking. The short-lived Nashua Watch Co. is another example.[62] There the inventors tried to go even further than Howard, who still considered some kind of handmade finishing to be an essential aspect for American-made watches. The Nashua group wanted to produce fully industrially but struggled with the financial necessities to fulfill this plan. Nevertheless, the story of Belding Dart Bingham, the founder of the Nashua Watch Co., who had worked for the Waltham Watch Company before, shows quite well that there was a specific group of people that shared their knowledge due to their experiences in the early period of American watchmaking. It is therefore not surprising that the Nashua Watch Co. was bought by Waltham again after its bankruptcy.

The combination of the knowledge and expertise of the two companies would eventually also be visible during the Philadelphia Centennial Exposition in 1876, when the Waltham Watch Co. presented the results of precise industrialized watchmaking that would shock Swiss watchmakers. The early companies had developed special movements, which set the standards for US watches in the years to come, namely Waltham's English-style full plate, Nashua's English-style 3/4-plate, and Howard's split-plate design. The "fundamental advantage of easy assembly"[63] would make the American production process much cheaper, and the Swiss watchmaking industry would therefore suffer a bitter blow in the late 19th century.

Millions of Americans would be able to have their own watch, and it had been the most important task for the early watch companies to find a way to produce this number of watches. It was consequently not the quality but the quantity of watches that had to be secured by research and development in this early period of the American system of watchmaking. Jewelers, who were also important as investors and sellers as a consequence, could "sell their watch movements, along with fitted silver cases made to go with them. Jewelers assembled finished watches from the variety of standard-sized movements and casings."[64] From 1859, however, the watch cases could be produced much easier and cheaper, as James Boss had patented a new production method for them, leading to an increasing demand for movements to fill the cases.[65]

---

[62] Thomas De Fazio, "The Nashua Venture and The American Watch Company," *Bulletin of the National Association of Watch and Clock Collectors, Inc.* 17, no. 6 (1975): 574-589.
[63] Harrold, *American Watchmaking*, 25.
[64] McCrossen, *Marking Modern Times*, 59.
[65] Patent US23820A.

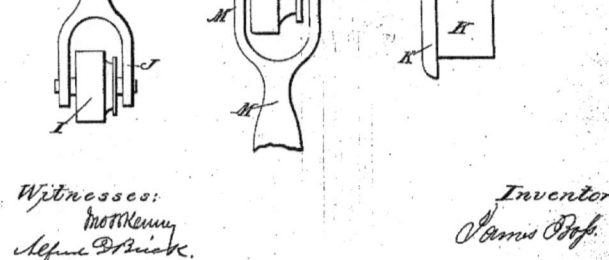

Fig. 1.14: Images from Boss's Patent, 1859, Pocket Watch Database.[66]

From the early 1860s, it was consequently possible to industrially produce large quantities of watches, and common households were therefore able to buy these American-made products. And while there were only two companies

---

[66] PD-US. Accessed May 12, 2021. https://pocketwatchdatabase.com/reference/patent/23820/watch-case-mfg.

that produced watches at that time—the American Watch Co. and E. Howard & Co.—it was the experience of the Civil War that stimulated not only an interest in watches but also the establishment of several other American watch companies. Jones had grown up in this first period of American watchmaking and had gathered knowledge and experience while he worked for Howard in Boston, but it was the Civil War that probably made him realize that there could be a chance to turn his skills into a fortune.

2.
The Civil War, Jones, and the Birth of an Idea

The watch industry and its advancements and growth were impacted in many ways by the US Civil War, and in 1870, *Appleton's Journal of Literature, Science and Art* claimed the story of American watchmaking to be a success story: "The American watch has eminent claims as the true republican heirloom—a triumph of industry in an age of industry, it symbolized the progress and dignity of labor; a product of American enterprise, it is associated with the sentiment of patriotism; moderate in cost, it is accessible to the body of the people, and, thoroughly made, it is prepared for a lengthened future."[1] Indeed, for the industry, the war had been a real "takeoff moment" as it spread knowledge about watches and increased demand, such that the business of producing and selling watches eventually became even more attractive for further investments. The fact that soldiers were eventually leaving their uniforms behind but not their pocket watches, which they had become familiar with during the war years, meant an increasing spread of knowledge about as well as desire for new watches across the United States. While watches had remained a limited phenomenon during the US-Mexican War (1846-48),[2] when it was mostly officers who were the ones carrying watches, now it had become more like a mass phenomenon, and the pocket watch would attract many new customers and future watch lovers.

Most of the soldiers had to begin carrying watches to follow the necessary time discipline that had been demanded in relation to their military duties. The Civil War caused large armies to confront each other on a larger geographical and more extended time scale, which is why watches were essential to synchronize the actions of the soldiers that participated in it. The coordination of military processes consequently demanded that more and more men had

---

[1] Cited in McCrossen, *Marking Modern Times*, 63.
[2] In contrast to the Civil War experience of many US soldiers, the US-Mexican War instead remained an imagined war for a majority of the American population. Jason Ahlenius, "Sensation's Imperial Narratives: Affect in the United States' Democracy of Print, 1846–1848," *Western American Literature* 50, no. 4 (2016): 285-315.

access to time and the possibility to act according to it.³ Coordinated actions and better and more widespread planning were necessary at the start of battles, and therefore, initially, more and more officers, whose uniforms were designed to allow them to carry a watch quite prominently as some kind of essential tool, got watches, but their example was quickly imitated by the soldiers of the lower ranks as well. What the railroad had stimulated on the civil level, the Civil War did on the military one. The increasing demand of both fields would have a positive impact on the development of the American watch industry, although the Civil War really created a massive demand for watches, and some kind of gold rush pushed the industry forward considerably both while and after the Union and the Confederate States fought over the future of the country and nation.

Possessing a watch became an essential aspect of military service for many men between 1861 and 1865, and these items were sent as presents from the home front to the field or vice versa. The soldiers consequently acted as synergetic actors who spread knowledge about the new technology from the battlefield to American homes, where their reports sparked an interest in possessing a pocket watch as well. Many soldiers would return from the war with their watch—these had been shipped directly to the front by retailers—and thereby bring modern timepieces even to rather rural areas of the post-war era. The veteran consequently became a replicator of the increased wartime interest and kept the demand for watches high in the post-war years as well.

That the urge to possess a watch was quite intensive for many soldiers can be emphasized by the fact that many of them not only directly ordered watches for themselves, but often even more watches to sell on to other soldiers from their unit as well. Watches were obviously not only a good trade item, but also something that troops on both sides looted from prisoners of war or dead bodies to address their own desire for pocket watches.

The steadily growing demand for pocket watches also helped jewelers, who would sell many watches as middlemen, putting the movements they bought from the watch companies into cases to match the customers' demand. Military memorabilia expressing pride in the cause of each opposing side or showing important national images, like flags or eagles, regional symbols, etc. were quite popular. Jewelers and watchmakers in the US prospered during the war as a consequence of these trends and would come up with all kinds of designs to match the possible wishes of their military customers. Eventually, it

---

[3] J.P. Clark, *Preparing for War: The Emergence of the Modern U.S. Army, 1815-1917* (Cambridge, MA: Harvard University Press, 2017), 99-128.

was clear that, as Alexis McCrossen worded it, "the pocket watch was an indispensable part of the self-made American's tool kit."[4] It was a symbol for the social advancement of many, a new, self-confident and growing middle class, as well as an industry that produced more and more watches to eventually give almost everyone a chance to get their hands on a quality timepiece at a relatively low cost. Watches thereby became the new symbols of status, replacing guns, pistols or knives in a way, and images of Civil War soldiers and later veterans, like the photograph above assumably showing Jones, show that watches had become an essential element of self-inscenation.

Fig. 2.1: Unidentified soldier, possibly Private Florentine Ariosto Jones of Co. A, 13th Massachusetts Infantry Regiment, in Union uniform with pocket watch, Library of Congress.[5]

---

[4] McCrossen, *Marking Modern Times*, 64.
[5] Accessed May 12, 2021. https://www.loc.gov/pictures/item/2012649879/.

The pocket watch was an important element to personalize time and the relationship people could have with it while, at the same moment, also emphasizing their own social rank within American society. It also offered a possibility, as mentioned before, to display some form of symbolism, particularly a patriotic dedication to the reunified nation after 1865. Watch cases could be engraved appropriately and at the same time also allowed those who owned a watch to separate it from mass-produced items by this kind of personal touch. The industry realized the chances the war had provided, and it is not surprising that a wave of new investments in watch companies was the consequence of the steadily increasing demand for pocket watches from soldiers and other people across the country during the war years. The American Watch Co. was experiencing what Michael C. Harrold correctly referred to as "one of the most prosperous growth periods in its long history."[6]

As mentioned before, the market had long been dominated by Swiss-manufactured pocket watches, but during the Civil War, Waltham's market share increased to 20%, and the American Watch Company's success during the early 1860s stimulated a rush for the foundation of new watch companies in the United States, especially since prices had increased by 25% during the Civil War as well. In 1863, the American Watch Co. had already produced 38,000 movements, meaning an average of around 150 per working day.[7] In addition to these, Swiss imports still counted for 226,000 watches, while the import of English timepieces had declined to merely 30,000 watches. At the same time, there was a boom for watch repairs and the sales for used watches because almost everyone seemed to have realized their own need to possess a timepiece that would be as individual as possible.

It is therefore not surprising that five new watch companies and competitors for the American Watch Company's success had been established in 1864, namely:

- National Watch Company, Elgin, IL
- Newark Watch Company, Newark, NJ
- United States Watch Company, Newark, NJ
- Tremont Watch Company, Boston, MA
- New York Watch Company, Providence, RI

---

[6] Harrold, *American Watchmaking*, 27.

[7] On Waltham's American Watch Company, see Henry G. Abbott, *History of the American Waltham Watch Company of Waltham, Mass.* (Exeter, NH: Adams Brown Co., 1968).

Fig. 2.2: 19th-century watch dealer's business card with Elgin logo, Boston Public Library.[8]

---

[8] PD-US. Accessed May 12, 2021. https://www.wikiwand.com/en/Elgin_National_Watch_Company.

Fig. 2.3: United States Watch Co., Newark, NJ, Pocket Watch Database.[9]

Although only Tremont Watch Co. was actually able to start selling watches before the end of the war, this number clearly shows the potential gains many of the people involved in these companies expected from selling watches in the mid-1860s. It was mainly people involved in the jewels trade who had been acting as investors in all companies. While they had bought foreign watches before and put them into cases and sold the finished product, these men now wanted to control the whole trade and sell their own watches, increasing their margin as well, of course.

The wartime demand had created fortunes for the jewelers, who now used the money to invest heavily in the new companies that were supposed to increase the income of investors and manufacturers even further. Most of the newly established watch companies needed years to deal with the preparations for production, as they needed machinery, designs, skilled workers, and many other things, which is why the war was already over before four of the five new brands could actually be purchased by customers who wanted to buy a new pocket watch. In the end, all but one went bankrupt rather fast, as they were unable to repay their debts quickly once the war was over. This, however, also showed how expensive the innovative process to apply an American system of watchmaking was, and it was almost tragic that Jones's plan in Switzerland would suffer from similar issues. In contrast to the US firms, however, he hoped to find more skilled labor in Europe as the companies that were established

---

[9] PD-US. Accessed May, 12, 2021. https://pocketwatchdatabase.com/assets/images/history/united-states-watch-factory-marion.jpg.

during the Civil War had also struggled with limitations of sufficient skilled workers. Usually, when a company was going bankrupt, it would not take long until its workforce was absorbed by another competing watch company. The ones that survived the cash-intensive transformation process in the US would eventually dominate the market there and even replace the watches that had been imported before.

It was nevertheless not only watch production that had increased, but also that of cases and other relevant accessories, and, with one eye on Waltham, *The Jewelers Circular and Horological Review* reflected upon the developments after the Civil War as follows:

> In the early days of watch-making, and indeed up to the advent of the American machine-made watch, each movement had its case made expressly for it, and the one manufacturer was responsible for both. Each made up the complete watch, and [the] maker's name guaranteed both the excellence of the movement and the quality of the case. American watch-making has changed all that. The manufacturer of movements and cases is now divided between entirely separate branches of business. They are held separately by their manufacturers, and are put together to make a watch by the dealers—usually the retail dealers. ... It [the combination of trades in the American system of watchmaking, F.J.] has enabled the consumer to reap the advantages of having both parts of his watch made in quantity at the low prices which can only be afforded by manufacturing on a wholesale scale. ... The WALTHAM WATCH COMPANY has been enabled to combine the advantages of both these systems, avoiding the drawbacks of both. It is the only company which makes silver cases for its own movements, and it makes them in its own factory.[10]

Regardless of their later success or failure, the new companies and their competition to produce as fast as possible continued to stimulate the eventual formation of the American system of watchmaking that would be able to produce pocket watches in the United States on an industrial scale. This process was made possible by the involvement of big capital and people who were willing to support skilled manufacturers and their ideas to reach unknown modes of production as fast as possible. Thereby, at the end of the Civil War, "pioneering was ending and profiteering had begun."[11]

---

[10] *The Jewelers Circular and Horological Review* 5, no. 10, November 16, 1874: 167.
[11] Harrold, *American Watchmaking*, 34.

Fig. 2.4: Waltham Watch Co. advertisement, 1890s.[12]

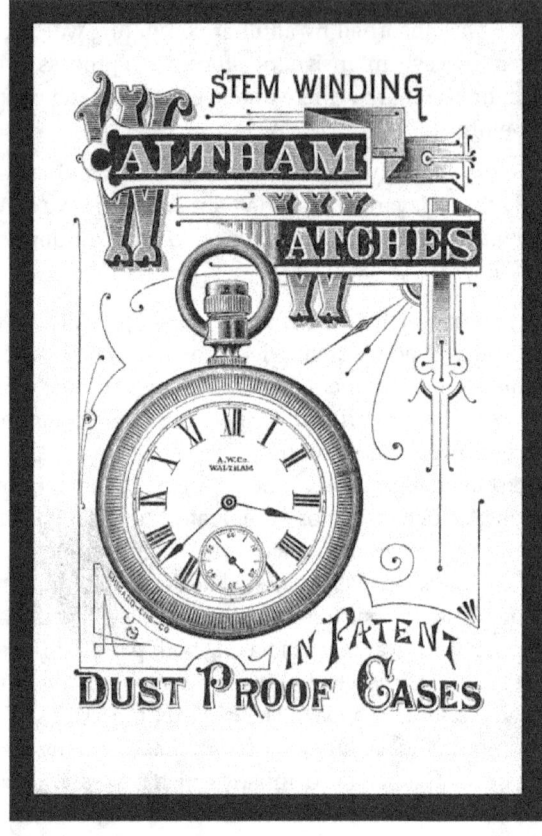

In the mid-1860s, watch companies were able to produce a diversity of new items, namely

1) precision timekeepers;
2) complicated watches such as chronographs;
3) inexpensive jeweled watches;
4) cheap unjeweled watches;
5) stem-winding and setting;
6) nickel damaskeening;
7) smaller watches for both ladies and gentlemen;
8) thinner watches.[13]

---

[12] PD-US. Accessed May 12, 2021. https://stricklandvintagewatches.com/waltham-watch-company-advertisement-circa-1890/.
[13] Ibid., 34-35.

By the time of the aforementioned Philadelphia Centennial Exposition, US watch companies were able to mass-produce all kinds of watch parts and elements and therefore could offer cheap watches without losing quality. This was the true and sensational achievement of the American watch system which shocked foreign competitors when its efficiency was publicly displayed for the first time.

Regardless of the eventual successes, many who attempted to gain from the demands for watches from the early 1860s failed, but there are personal continuities within the watch trade that demonstrate how knowledge and skills as well as experience in building and selling timepieces were passed along. John C. Adams, to name just one example, was involved in the establishment of five watch companies, including Elgin, and whenever a new company tried to compete in the watch business, they would also compete for skilled workers. The watch industry was consequently well connected with many personal overlaps in the history of the different companies. The ones that had been founded during the Civil War would disappear relatively fast again, and examples like the Newark Watch Co. or the Cornell Watch Co. would not live long enough to leave a mark. Nevertheless, Paul Cornell, who had founded the latter, had similar ideas with regard to cheap labor to Jones. However, Cornell did not intend to move production out of the country but rather thought about moving it to the West Coast, namely San Francisco, where he assumed he would be able to use cheaper Chinese-American labor for his watch production instead. However, this idea never saw the light of day because Cornell went bankrupt before it could be realized.

All of those who wanted to be successful at selling watches on the American market therefore had to be aware of a few things, and if they were ignored, the attempt to establish a successful watch company was doomed from its start. One needed 1) larger sums of capital, 2) new models to gain a foothold in the market, and 3) innovative ideas to gain ground against almost almighty competitors like Waltham's American Watch Co. that were already building and selling all kinds of watches at a high quality for a low price by the 1870s. This, however, does not mean that watchmakers in the United States were the only ones that invested in research and development, although they might eventually have been more successful in applying its results into establishing a truly modern watch industry. And even in the decade after the Civil War, Swiss watch manufacturers sold relatively high numbers of watches: more than 2.5 million were exported to the US. That Swiss watch exports remained high was due to the fact that labor was cheap in Switzerland and high-quality timepieces could therefore be assembled for a competitive price. In contrast to their English competitors, Swiss watches continued to play a role in the American market, and jewelers or retailers would import movements at low prices to finish and sell in the United States. With higher production rates—Waltham and Elgin produced ca. 100,000 movements per year from the mid-1870s[14]—prices began to drop, and in the late 1870s, a price war began that only the larger companies could survive. In this regard, the market determined the fate of many companies, and in Switzerland, Jones would suffer from this American price war as well, because his International Watch Company needed to compete with the US competition.

It seems to be time to take a closer look at Jones and how his idea to establish a watch company that would produce watches in Switzerland but sell them on the US market took shape during and immediately after the Civil War. There is not a lot we can say with certainty about Jones. Born in Romney, New Hampshire, "a local center for milling and tanning,"[15] he lived with his parents, Solomon (1797-1864), a shoemaker, and Lavinia, as well as with his elder brother Greenleaf (1834-1908). Seyffer assumes that Jones's first and middle names referenced the city of Florence and the popular poet Ludovico Ariosto (1474-1533) and that his "parents chose the names in the hope that their son would lead a life that was both creative and adventurous,"[16] but there is no proof for these assumptions. Jones's family had connections to the watch industry early on, as his two grand-uncles, Levi and Abel Hutchins, had previously worked as clockmakers in New Hampshire. It has been speculated that Jones might have started his apprenticeship by working for his grand-uncles, but this can neither be confirmed nor denied. The fact remains, however, that there were some connections to the clock trade early on. There is also a rumor that Jones joined the Boston Watch Co. in the second half of the 1850s, but there is no real proof for this speculation either. However, it is a fact that Jones must have learned watchmaking somewhere and lived in Boston by the time the Civil War began.[17]

According to his pension and military records, Jones was enlisted on 24 July 1861 and served until he was honorably discharged on 1 August 1864 as private of Company A, 13th Massachusetts Infantry Regiment.[18] Although initially drafted for minor military duties, Jones's regiment would participate in some

---

[14] McCrossen, *Marking Modern Times*, 77.
[15] Seyffer, "Watchmaking," 21.
[16] Ibid.
[17] Ibid., 22.
[18] Pension and military records re. F.A. Jones, IWC Archive, DC 04-26/28. The original can be found at: Susan P. Jones, Pension Records, National Archives and Records Administration (NARA), Washington, D.C. and Florentine Ariosto Jones, Military Service Records, NARA.

major battles of the Civil War.[19] Initially, the Massachusetts Volunteers had been assigned to patrol duties on the Upper Potomac River, and its soldiers first saw combat action in West Virginia in September 1861. In August 1862, the regiment took part in the Battle of Cedar Mountain,[20] the Battle of Thoroughfare Gap,[21] and the Second Battle of Bull Run.[22] After some other battle engagements, the 13th Massachusetts Infantry Regiment fought at the Battle of Fredricksburg in Virginia in mid-December.[23] In the following year, the regiment would also participate in the Battle of Gettysburg[24] in early July, as well as the Bristoe Campaign[25] and the Mine Run Campaign.[26] Before the men of the regiment were eventually mustered out in August 1864, they would continue to fight in several battles and campaigns and were also involved in the Siege of Petersburg[27] from mid-June to mid-July of that year.

Jones, according to Seyffer, was "clearly not cut out for a military career,"[28] but his experiences during the war were twofold. He had seen what level of destruction could be achieved in modern warfare, and further to the 161 men who had died in service during the 13th Massachusetts Infantry Regiment's engagement in the Civil War, many had come home with invisible wounds to

---

[19] Charles E. Davis, *Three Years in the Army: The Story of the Thirteenth Massachusetts Volunteers from July 16, 1861 to August 1, 1864* (Boston: Estes and Lauriat, 1894).

[20] Kanisorn Wangsrichanalai, "Battle of Cedar Mountain," *Encyclopedia Virginia*, January 12, 2016. Accessed November 10, 2020. http://www.EncyclopediaVirginia.org/Cedar_Mountain_Battle_of. Also see Robert K. Krick, *Stonewall Jackson at Cedar Mountain* (Chapel Hill, NC: University of North Carolina Press, 1990).

[21] John J. Hennessy, *Return to Bull Run: The Campaign and Battle of Second Manassas* (New York: Simon & Schuster, 1993), 154-160.

[22] David G. Martin, *The Second Bull Run Campaign: July–August 1862* (New York: Da Capo Press, 1997).

[23] Gary W. Gallagher, ed. *The Fredericksburg Campaign: Decision on the Rappahannock* (Chapel Hill, NC: University of North Carolina Press, 1995); Francis Augustín O'Reilly, *The Fredericksburg Campaign: Winter War on the Rappahannock* (Baton Rouge, LA: Louisiana State University Press, 2003).

[24] Mark Adkin, *The Gettysburg Companion: The Complete Guide to America's Most Famous Battle* (Mechanicsburg, PA: Stackpole Books, 2008); Allen C. Guelzo, *Gettysburg: The Last Invasion* (New York: Knopf, 2013).

[25] William D. Henderson, *The Road to Bristoe Station: Campaigning with Lee and Meade, August 1–October 20, 1863* (Lynchburg, VA: H. E. Howard, 1987).

[26] Martin F. Graham, and George F. Skoch, *Mine Run: A Campaign of Lost Opportunities, October 21, 1863–May 1, 1864* (Lynchburg, VA: H. E. Howard, 1987).

[27] Earl Hess, *In the Trenches at Petersburg: Field Fortifications and Confederate Defeat* (Chapel Hill, NC: The University of North Carolina Press, 2009).

[28] Seyffer, "Watchmaking," 22.

their souls. At the same time, Jones had realized the impact of modern watchmaking and witnessed the trends and developments described above first hand. It must have been during his active service that he thought about the idea to found a watch company of his own for the first time.

Fig. 2.5: The army of the Potomac at Mine Run – General Warren's troops attacking, *Harper's Weekly*, 1 January 1864.[29]

After his military service, Jones seems, as far as company records allow us to tell, to have worked for E. Howard in Boston before he left the company again in 1867 or 1868.[30] Howard, nevertheless, ran a company that still produced quality than rather quantity, and the company records do not show any sign that Howard produced more watches after the war than before.[31] Regardless of Howard's policy with regard to production, Jones must have been able to learn everything he needed there about the precise production of watch parts and realized, if he had not already fully done so during his military service, that a watch company could be a promising and very successful business idea. At E. Howard's watch factory, Jones "very quickly climbed the career ladder"[32] and eventually became the Chief Assistant and Superintendent there. Since Howard had also worked with Dennison, it is likely that Jones was inspired not only by

---

[29] PD-US. Accessed May, 12, 2021. https://commons.wikimedia.org/wiki/File:Harper%27s_Weekly_-_Battle_of_Mine_Run_-_Gen._Warren%27s_Troops_Attacking.jpg.
[30] E. Howard Clock Co. Records, The National Museum of American History, Archives Center, Washington, D.C., Collection No. 776, Box 1, December 1862-January 30, 1866.
[31] E. Howard Clock Co. Records, The National Museum of American History, Archives Center, Washington, D.C., Collection No. 776, Box 1, September 2, 1868-November 17, 1869.
[32] Seyffer, "Watchmaking," 24.

Howard's success but also by the ideas Dennison had brought to the table. Jones therefore witnessed the genesis of new watch companies during the Civil War, like the National Watch Co. in Chicago, which would later become the Elgin National Watch Co., and his own idea for the International Watch Company in Schaffhausen also took shape, maybe especially due to his talks with Howard or Dennison. Jones was probably "infected" by the euphoria of so many men in the watch business and supposedly had an idea that would circumvent some of the problems in that time period, particularly the lack of skilled and cheap labor. In addition, Jones dreamed big and did not want to stay at Howard's company while other watch companies began to produce massive amounts of watches for a market that seemed to have an unlimited appetite for them.

What, however, is strange and still cannot be answered is the question of where Jones got the money for his plan. While the IWC still likes to stress the idea of a man with a dream and guts, who founded his own watch company in Schaffhausen to produce American-inspired Swiss-built watches, it is hardly true that Jones could achieve all this without some capital investment from others who, nevertheless, still remain unknown today. Howard soon lost ground to the National Watch Co., and Dennison once more tried his luck in catching up with the latter by founding the Tremont Watch Co. It is interesting that he also thought about producing some parts for his watches in Switzerland to save on costs, and the imported parts would be combined with ones produced in Boston.[33] Dennison's investors, first and foremost, the jeweler A. O. Bigelow of Bigelow, Kennard & Co., however, were not persuaded by this idea and continued to produce all their parts in the US. Jones, on the other hand, might have got his inspiration from Dennison and probably found some investors who were willing to support his plan for an outsourcing of expensive labor. Dennison eventually left the Tremont Watch Co. and later successfully produced watch cases near Birmingham, England, which were sold worldwide and became a landmark in the jewelry trade. Dennison's story shows that an outsourcing of labor-intensive production to cheaper countries could be a success, yet Jones wanted to build watch movements, not cases, although the basic idea of the two men was the same: produce important parts and sell them to the US, where they would simply be assembled and sold at a competitive price range.

Jones had the skills, which he had learned in the early watch industry and in his years before leaving for Switzerland at Howard's factory. He consequently took Dennison's approach much further when he intended to produce finished movements that would be sold on the US market. The question about Jones's possible network of investors and business partners is something that could

---

[33] Harrold, *American Watchmaking*, 32.

not have been constructed yet, but there are some aspects that highlight that the young American probably did not act as a lone darer, but was rather backed by some prominent men in the watch and jewelers trade. In 1868, the same year Jones began his work in Switzerland, the Philadelphia Watch Co. was founded by Eugene Paulus. While the company marketed watches that looked quite similar to Howard's watches, an actual production site could never be identified.[34] Due to the timely coincidence, one could argue that Jones and Paulus might have worked together in selling Jones's Swiss watches under the coverage of an American company, but this also must remain speculative at this point.

What is even more interesting and also points to Jones acting on behalf of a group of investors and American businessmen is the fact that, in March 1868, shortly before he began his work in Switzerland, Jones was initiated as a freemason into the Lodge of Washington.[35] This could only have been possible with somebody vouching for Jones, and it is also obvious that the young man joined the lodge for a more business-oriented reason. In 1867, Jones had been in Europe and might have realized that a lodge membership could help him with his business plans, especially since a masonic lodge by the name of Akazia had existed in Winterthur, only about 18 miles away from Schaffhausen, since 1820.[36] Whatever the reason for his membership of the Lodge of Washington might have been, it was only possible because Jones had had support during the initiation procedures.

In Schaffhausen, however, there was only a lodge of the Independent Order of Odd Fellows (IOOF), Rheinfall-Lodge No. 9, which resembled many aspects related to masonic lodges, yet did not have any direct ties to freemasonry. Furthermore, this lodge was not established before 1877, although its early members might have been men Jones could have had an exchange with.[37] The man behind the foundation of this IOOF lodge was the wine dealer Franz Stahel, who gathered friends and supporters on 4 July 1877, when the lodge was

---

[34] William Muir, "The Problem of Chestnut Street," *Bulletin of the National Association of Watch & Clock Collectors* 13, no. 11 (1969): 1019-1021.

[35] Massachusetts, Mason Membership Cards, 1733-1990. New England Historic Genealogical Society. I would like to thank Judy Lacey, Archivist at the New England Historic Genealogical Society, who helped me to find and identify Jones's record.

[36] Freimaurerloge Akazia, ed. *200 Jahre Freimaurerloge Akazia Winterthur* (Winterthur: K-Edition, 2020).

[37] Festschrift zum 100jährigen Bestehen und Wirken der Rheinfall-Loge Nr. 9 des Schweizerischen Odd Fellow-Bundes in Schaffhausen, 1977, StdA SH.

officially established as the ninth IOOF lodge in Switzerland.[38] Regardless of the fact that Rheinfall-Lodge No. 9 was not a masonic one, Jones might have had contact with its early members (Tab. 2.1.) while he was in Schaffhausen himself.

Table 2.1.: Members initiated into Rheinfall-Lodge No. 9 in 1877/78.[39]

Membership No.	Name, Profession, and Place of Residence	Date of Initiation
1	Franz Stahel, Wine dealer, Schaffhausen	20 June 1877
2	Gustav Basler, Railway officer, Schaffhausen	20 June 1877
3	Jakob Müller, Merchant, Schaffhausen	20 June 1877
4	Walter Vogt, Wine dealer for Stahel & Vogt, Schaffhausen	20 June 1877
5	Caspar Uehli, Bank cashier, Schaffhausen	26 June 1877
6	Alexander Bolli, District commander, Schaffhausen	8 December 1877
7	Heinrich Vogler, Employee, Schaffhausen	8 December 1877
8	Wilhelm Heim, Merchant, Schaffhausen	8 December 1877
9	Carl Lauffer, Merchant, Schaffhausen	8 December 1877
10	Bernhard Kehlhofer, Forester, Schaffhausen	8 December 1877
11	Johann Wildi, Merchant, Zurich	11 December 1877
12	Jonas Gideon, Merchant, Zurich	11 December 1877
13	Ernst Müller-Fink, City councillor, Schaffhausen	15 January 1878

Regardless of the truth, which probably cannot be reconstructed without further sources, a few things can be emphasized at the end of this chapter. Jones had realized during the Civil War and his time working for the E. Howard Watch Co. in Boston that there was an enormous demand for watches that could be produced in large numbers and for a cheap retail price. At the same time, he developed Dennison's idea further to outsource the production process to

---

[38] Rudolf Spörri, "Rheinfall-Loge Nr.9 Schaffhausen," in *100 Jahre Odd-Fellow-Orden in der Schweiz 1871-1971*, ed. Oskar Glaus (Wimmis: Odd-Fellow-Bund, 1971), 115-119, here 115.

[39] Otto Dolder, *Geschicht der Rheinfall-Loge Nr. 9 I.O.O.F. Schaffhausen 1877-1927*, n.p., 1927, StdA SH, Bro 1242.

Switzerland, where skilled workers seemed to be available for a cheaper salary than in the US. Jones was also well prepared to use both existent networks and such that could be instrumentalized for his own purposes. Regardless of acting as a single daring individual or a representative for a larger network of US investors, Jones was definitely willing to take the risk of founding his own watch business in Switzerland. This venture will now be discussed in its Swiss context to show how Jones went on to make his ideas see the light of day in Schaffhausen.

3.
Jones and the International Watch Company

It was Jones's experience during the war, his time at Howard's watch company, and maybe the inspiration he received from his trip to Europe and talks with Dennison about Switzerland that stimulated his decision to move there to establish his own watch company. This company was supposed to apply the American system of watchmaking and sell its products on the American market, gaining an advantage with regard to low retail prices as a consequence of lower wage costs, and it could thereby produce high-quality timepieces relatively cheaply to guarantee high margins of money would be made. In the present chapter, I will provide a survey about the Swiss context of this venture and describe how Jones brought his dream to life in Schaffhausen before discussing and analyzing the reasons for his eventual failure in some detail.

3.1. The Swiss Context

There had been a long tradition of watchmaking in Switzerland before Jones even set foot on Swiss soil. What the American watchmaker underestimated in a way is the fact that watch manufacturing there "was and still is a traditional, if not a conservative craft."[1] There was hardly any industrial production of watches before Jones arrived with his idea to apply the American system of watchmaking to produce a massive number of watches with interchangeable parts that had also been produced by machines.[2] Nevertheless, Jones would start a new development within Swiss watchmaking and, from a long-term perspective, would pave the way for the success of the watch industry in Switzerland in the years that followed his failed attempt. Although the present work focuses on Jones, he was nevertheless alone with regard to this

---

[1] Seyffer, "Watchmaking," 7. On watchmaking in German-speaking Switzerland, see Georg von Holtey, Ursula Bischof Scherer and Albert Kägi, *Deutschschweizer Uhrmachermeister und ihre Werke vom 14. bis 19. Jahrhundert* (La Chaux-de-Fonds: Chronométrophilia, 2006). On the historical developments in the region around Neuchâtel, see Estelle Fallet and Alain Cortat, *Apprendre l'horlogerie dans le Montagnes neuchâteloises, 1740-1810* (La Chaux-de-Fonds: Institut l'Homme et le Temps, 2001).

[2] Seyffer, *Die Unternehmensgeschichte*, 55.

development, as many other Swiss watch entrepreneurs would play important roles as well to pave the way for the steady success of Swiss Watchmaking from the mid-19th century to the 21st century, e.g. Ernest Francillon (1834-1900, Longines),[3] Nicolas G. Hayek (1928-2010, Swatch Group) and Jean-Claude Biver (Hublot).[4] The modernization of the watch industry in Switzerland and the "Americanization" of its production processes, was without any doubt a collective process,[5] and companies like Longines[6] or Omega[7] maybe played a more important role with regard to its long-term success than Jones and the early IWC, but it can nevertheless emphasize, that some of the earliest attempts to apply American production methods had been made in Schaffhausen by the young man the present study intends to focus on, and who realized the necessity for bold decisions long before most of the other decisive figures in the watch trade. The shock Swiss watchmakers felt when they realized that US watchmakers had left their competition behind when the latter displayed the capacities of the American system of watchmaking in Philadelphia in 1876 would eventually cause the Swiss watchmakers to think more intensely about Jones and his ideas, even though his watch company had failed by that time.

Before Jones attempted to change the overall structure of Swiss watchmaking, it was dominated by the so-called "établissage" system (assembling system) that was dominated by a network of home workers, a division of labor, and an effective production system that was made possible due to the low costs of labor. This system was controlled by the établisseurs, who would eventually collect the watch parts, put them together, and sell the final product.[8] Although this system had been applied in large parts of Switzerland when Jones first arrived, the place that was usually referred to as the birthplace of Swiss watchmaking was Geneva, where Calvinist artisans like goldsmiths, jewelers,

---

[3] Pierre César, *Ernest Francillon: Sa vie et son oeuvre* (Saint-Imier: Longines, 1992).

[4] Pierre-Yves Donzé, "Industrial Leadership and the Long-Lasting Competitiveness of the Swiss Watch Industry," in *Historians on Leadership and Strategy: Case Studies From Antiquity to Modernity*, ed. Martin Gutmann (Cham: Springer, 2019), 171-191.

[5] Christophe Koller, *L'industrialisation et l'état au pays de l'horlogerie: Contribution à l'histoire économique et sociale d'une région suisse* (Courrendlin: Editions Communication jurassienne et européenne (CJE), 2003).

[6] Laurent Giauque, Vincent Guggisberg, and Christian Milz, *Longines*, 2. vols. (Neuchâtel: [Université de Neuchâtel Division économique et sociale, 1988); Patrick Linder, *Longines, un sablier et des ailes: Histoire, enjeux, construction d'une marque: 120 ans de la protection d'un logotype (1889-2009)* (Saint-Imier: Editions des Longines, 2009).

[7] John Goldberger, *Omega Watches* (Bologna: Damiani, 2005); Marco Richon, *Omega: The History of a Great Brand* (Bienne, Switzerland: Omega SA, 1994).

[8] Seyffer, "Innovation oder Nachahmung?" 12.

etc. had also played an important role.⁹ Although the city soon advanced to become a center of the watch trade, it was not a site for production because constituent parts, as has been mentioned above, were often produced in small villages by a large number of home workers.¹⁰ However, the city played an important role in the development of watchmaking in Switzerland.

The first Swiss watchmaker guild was founded in Geneva in 1601. For the next one and a half centuries, the watch trade would remain centered in the city, which was an important part of the jewelry trade in central Europe as well. It was after the 1750s that the demand for watches increased and manufacturing in Switzerland began to spread to other regions. For the artisans, the watch was first and foremost a product for export, which is why cheap production was their main interest. Initially, aesthetics were also more important than functionality, which is why relatively fancy looking but overall cheap watches could be produced.¹¹ They often used French-style movements as they were easy to manufacture, and since France was one of the export markets in Europe as well, this practice made sense. In France, on the other hand, it was Frédéric Japy (1749-1812) who first tried to produce watches in higher numbers, and he set up a factory in 1770. Ten years later, he was able to manufacture 20,000 raw movements per year, and he had doubled this number by 1795.

In 1805, his factory produced 180,000 movements, a number that would increase further and, by 1813, it had reached 300,000.¹²

---

[9] Seyffer, *Die Unternehmensgeschichte*, 58; Seyffer, "Watchmaking," 9. See also Estelle Fallet, Musée Rath et al., *Watchmaking in Geneva: The Magic of Craftsmanship* (Geneva: Musées d'art et d'histoire, 2011) and Salon international de la haute horlogerie, *La haute horlogerie genevoise, des origines au Poinçon de Genève de 1886* (Geneva: Salon international de la haute horlogerie, 2011).

[10] Albert Hauser, *Schweizerische Wirtschafts- und Sozialgeschichte* (Erlenbach-Zürich / Stuttgart: Eugen Rentsch Verlag, 1961), 223. On the system of home work, see also Adolf Blind, *Die Heimarbeit in der Schweiz* (Jena: Fischer 1929); Jacob Lorenz, *Die wirtschaftlichen und sozialen Verhältnisse in der schweiz. Heimarbeit: mit besonderer Berücksichtigung der Ergebnisse der schweizerischen Heimarbeit-Ausstellung* (Zurich: Kommissionsverlag der Buchhandlung des Schweiz. Grütlivereins, 1911) and Martin Schreck, "Die gewerbliche und kunstgewerbliche Heimarbeit in den Gebirgsgegenden der Schweiz und die mit ihr zusammenhängende Produktion für den eigenen Bedarf" (Dissertation Thesis, University of Bern, 1957).

[11] Harrold, *American Watchmaking*, 8.

[12] Seyffer, "Watchmaking," 14. On Japy, see Ivan Grassias et al., *Sur les traces de l'empire Japy* (Salins-les-Bains: Musées des techniques et cultures comtoises, 2001) and Pierre Lamard, *Frédéric Japy et son héritage* (Belfort: Société belfortaine d'émulation, 1999).

Fig. 3.1.1: Frédéric Japy, Frédéric Japy, portrait, Musée Japy, Beaucourt.[13]

Japy did also sell his raw movements to Swiss établisseurs, who would then add their own parts to finish the product and eventually sell the watches. Although Japy's work was important, French watchmaking declined in the 19th century and would not play a major role again. All in all, old-fashioned production methods came under pressure, regardless of how low wage costs were, when watchmakers like Japy began to use machinery for the production of watch parts, something Jones later tried to achieve through the implementation of the American system of watchmaking in Schaffhausen. However, it was not only Jones who applied new methods in Switzerland; other watchmakers had experimented with new technologies and techniques as well, especially since they needed to export watches that could match the demands of the market. With watch prices falling, more of them had to be produced as cheaply as possible. While the canton of Neuchâtel was particularly productive,[14] other regions, like the Vallée de Joux, also began to produce watches for the international market during the 19th century.[15]

---

[13] PD-US. Accessed May 12, 2021. https://watch-wiki.org/index.php?title=Datei:Louis_Fr%C3%A9d%C3%A9ric_Japy.jpg.
[14] There were already 464 watchmakers recorded for Neuchâtel in 1752, rising to 686 in 1762 and 3,458 in 1792. Seyffer, *Die Unternehmensgeschichte*, 60.
[15] Seyffer, "Watchmaking," 11-15.

The respective cantonal governments also played an important role in the spread of watchmaking in Switzerland. Since few resources were needed to fabricate a high-end export good, many regions had an interest in a profitable watch trade. It is consequently not surprising that schools for future watchmakers were set up in the early 19th century, like in Geneva in 1824.[16] In addition, guilds' compulsoriness had been abandoned in the late 18th century, an act that very much stimulated a growth in the production of watches. Without guilds, the établisseurs were able to draft their contracts with home workers individually and did not have to follow any demands from the restrictive guild laws. This made the division of labor, which was so typical of Swiss watchmaking, possible and stimulated economic growth in numerous regions in Switzerland.[17] Technological changes were addressed by the watchmakers, and innovations, such as the ones provided by Japy, were not ignored, like they were in England, which would soon fall behind with its watch production. Japy had also developed some tools that could be particularly useful for Swiss watchmakers as well, and the latter did not hesitate to adopt them into their production procedures.[18]

Regardless of such innovative developments, the établissage system remained in action as it functioned well and continued to provide economic advantages. The home or cottage workers manufactured watch parts like springs, dials, cases, and ébauches (raw movements) that were collected by the établisseurs, who ran the businesses, and put together in their workshops before they were sold.[19] The cottage workers were essential for this system, and since many people gained from its existence, it was not questioned by the watch traders or the authorities.[20] What was established over the years was a network between the manufacturers who provided the single parts and the watchmakers who would later put the watches together before they went on sale. This collective form of production was quite successful and secured the success of Swiss exports in the international watch trade. The établisseurs were in control of it and ensured the smooth running of the system. With its division of labor to increase productivity and the partial application of innovative technology in the early 19th century, the Swiss watch industry went through similar processes to other economically important sectors.[21]

---

[16] Ibid., 11.
[17] Seyffer, *Die Unternehmensgeschichte*, 59.
[18] Harrold, *American Watchmaking*, 8.
[19] Seyffer, "Watchmaking," 9.
[20] Philippe Blanchard, *L'établissage: Étude historique d'un système de production horloger en Suisse (1750-1950)* (Chézard-Saint-Martin: Editions de la Chatière, 2011).
[21] Pierre-Yves Donzé, *Histoire de l'industrie horlogère suisse: De Jacques David à Nicolas Hayek (1850-2000)* (Neuchâtel: Ed. Alphil, 2009); Ulrich Pfister, "Die Entstehung des industriellen Unternehmertums in der Schweiz, 18.-19. Jahrhundert," *Zeitschrift für Unternehmensgeschichte* 43 (1997): 14-38.

Fig. 3.1.2: Fritz Zuber-Bühler (1822-1896), The Watchmaker and His Family.[22]

Although the établissage system was quite successful for a long time, it was also limiting the advancement of Swiss watchmaking as an actual industry, as "no organized manufacture of watches in large batches with uniform standards was possible."[23] At the same time, there was no real pressure to change this system of production, because Swiss watches could be produced at such low costs that a change in or development of existent procedures seemed simply unnecessary. Nevertheless, with regard to its high level of division of labor,

---

[22] Accessed May 12, 2021. http://www.amismih.ch/en/collection/gallery/detail.html?tx_sbportfolio_pi1%5Buid%5D=6&cHash=ac09e928d3e43563ccdd0303e94ced77.
[23] Seyffer, "Watchmaking," 10.

Swiss watch production had already achieved an advantage and was able to provide the international market with large amounts of quality but cheap pocket watches, which were then sold in massive quantities to the United States.

What Jones later attempted was to centralize the process in a factory and to use more machine-produced parts at the same time. He consequently intended to further industrialize a systemized production process by adding the American system of watchmaking to an already well-developed process. The établissage system had already stimulated the establishment of smaller production sites, where parts and raw movements had been produced to match the steady demand for such parts. Due to this process, labor got more and more divided as well as specialized. This also meant that the établisseurs gained from the existence of very specialized but at the same time relatively cheap skilled labor and could therefore survive for a long time in an increasingly globalized watch trade, in which low prices represented a chance to compete and sell more watches than others. This was not only possible due to the cheap production cost, but the wide variety of watches that could be produced in Switzerland that could easily match different demands expressed by the customers in foreign countries. All in all, it was a very decentralized process that could only be controlled and taken advantage of by an experienced établisseur, whose responsibility it was to connect all single elements to achieve the assembly of all necessary parts into one single watch as the final product.[24]

However, organized industrial mass production was not possible within the existent system, and Jones was the first who really seemed to be willing to change this in Switzerland, although he was not the only one, and not the only foreigner moving to Switzerland to become active in watch production there.[25] That he chose to establish his company there was also related to the availability of skilled manufacturers and workers, who had gained experience from their work within the établissage system. Hence the attempt to centralize a so far decentralized workforce would cause some issues that will be discussed in more detail later. Even before industrial mass production could begin in Switzerland, the production of watches had been quite substantial, considering that watchmakers in the Swiss Jura had produced around 120,000 watches in the 1840s. A third of them were gold watches, selling at CHF 150, while silver watches could be bought for CHF 20.[26] Although the prices were competitive enough to secure Swiss exporters a good number of sales, the net gains were

---

[24] Seyffer, *Die Unternehmensgeschichte*, 63.
[25] Johann Boillat, Anton Näf and Peter Hans Horn, "Jules Grossmann: Ein Eberswalder Uhrmacher in der Schweiz," *Eberswalder Jahrbuch* 26 (2018): 98-105.
[26] Ibid., 64; Seyffer, "Watchmaking," 11.

also quite high. This was made possible by the low income of the home workers that had been contracted for the établissage system. This, in a way, caused a problem. As long as Swiss établisseurs could make money, even with cheaper export prices for their goods being available, they were not inclined to change the existent system. It was therefore due to Jones's attempt that the first changes were actually applied, and the Philadelphia Centennial Expedition in 1876 shocked the watchmakers of Switzerland enough to eventually and broadly apply some of the developments Jones had in mind for watch production in Switzerland.

Before Jones established the International Watch Company, Swiss manufacturers would still gain a lot by the demand the Civil War had created. In Europe, the low prices had secured a leading position for Swiss watchmakers, as other competitors there had either not adjusted their production process or simply could not produce as cheaply as the Swiss watchmakers.[27] The latter exported a lot of watches to the United States as well, where customers demanded cheap watches in large numbers, especially due to the trends and developments described in the previous chapter. Initially, while US competitors still experimented with the American system of watchmaking, they could not match Swiss prices, but the watches imported from Switzerland were often also of lower quality and were consequently perceived as bad by the final customers. For them, eventually, Swiss watches were all seen as bad watches as they did not differentiate between cheap ones and quality, high price pocket watches from Switzerland.[28] Regardless of such perceptions, Swiss production grew, as did the worldwide watch trade during the first half of the 19th century. The global number of watches produced rose from 350,000-400,000 in around 1800 to 2.5 million in 1850, and Switzerland economically gained a lot from this trend, as some regions there "managed to increase [the] production of watches to an extraordinary level."[29]

The existence of skilled workers in the highly divided production system in Switzerland did not only motivate Jones to move there to establish his own pocket watch factory; other European watchmakers moved there as well to gain from the cheap but highly specialized labor force. Jules Jürgensen (1808-1877)[30]

---

[27] Harrold, *American Watchmaking*, 9.
[28] Seyffer, "Watchmaking," 10.
[29] Ibid., 11.
[30] Fernand Donzé, "Les Jürgensen, horlogers négociants, mécènes, notables loclois: Jules-Frédéric, dit Jules I (1808-1877), Jules-Frédéric-Urban, dit Jules II (1837-1894)," *Biographies neuchâteloises* 3 (2001): 218-222; Frédérique Vouga et al., *Les Jürgensen* (Neuchâtel: Nouvelle revue neuchâleloise, 1996).

and Henri Robert Ekegren (1823-1896)[31] from Denmark, as well as Edouard Koehn (1839-1908)[32] from Saxony, are only a few examples of this trend, and at the same time they also highlight that the watch business had turned into a truly transnational and eventually globalized venture. That Switzerland was central within it is not surprising as the small Central European country went through a specific form of industrialization, marked by a lack of natural resources and overpopulation in the countryside which allowed the watch trade to recruit cheap labor there. These preconditions were essential for the successful development of the établissage system of watchmaking, which allowed the Swiss watch entrepreneurs to export high-quality products without too much stress for the local economy. Since the small size of the country also demanded that larger external markets sell the final products too, Switzerland had been ambitious in acting as an export nation,[33] especially within the international watch trade.[34] Taken together, the existence of a skilled labor force, the liberal political system that stimulated progress, and successful investment from and management by local economic elites laid the foundation for the advancement of Swiss watchmaking and a world rank that it has never really lost until today.[35]

Next to the cotton textile business and the silk weavers, it was the watch manufacturers that not only profited from the division of labor but also from the non-existence of strict guild laws.[36] When Jones arrived in the late 1860s, he consequently found the Swiss watch trade and manufacturing to be in quite a good shape, as it was next to ready to move to industrialization. What had not been implemented yet was a serial production of watches, but Jones intended to change this by applying his experiences with the American system of watchmaking. He thereby attempted something that would not be achieved in Switzerland at large before the end of the 19th century, facing similar problems to the ones that would turn the early history of the IWC into a challenge for all people involved. Jones's project was thereby, in a way, an expression of its time, because his argument for moving to Switzerland was related to the fact that not

---

[31] "Henri Robert Ekegren," *Le Point*. Accessed December 1, 2020. https://www.lepoint.fr/montres/Magazine/Grand-horlogers/henri-robert-ekegren-03-12-2012-2018111_2978.php.
[32] Klaus Pöhlmann, "Edouard Koehn: Über eine Uhr auf seiner Spur," *Klassik Uhren* 20, no. 1 (1997): 26-33.
[33] Michael Bernergger, "Die Schweiz und die Weltwirtschaft," in *Die Schweiz in der Weltwirtschaft (15.-20. Jh.)* (Zurich: Chronos, 1990), 432.
[34] Seyffer, *Die Unternehmensgeschichte*, 56.
[35] Christoph Buchheim, *Industrielle Revolutionen: Langfristige Wirtschaftsentwicklung in Grossbritannien, Europa und in Übersee* (Munich: DTV, 1994), 95.
[36] Seyffer, *Die Unternehmensgeschichte*, 56-57.

all parts of a watch could be produced by machines in the mid-1860s, and for him, one option to cut production costs at this point in the watch's technological development was to move to a country where skilled labor was available at low costs. In addition, Jones could not have successfully started his business in the United States, as he lacked both capital and a skilled workforce. In Schaffhausen, he could probably find both by granting the people there a share of his dream. For a city in Switzerland that had not yet gained so much from the Swiss watch trade, his offer seemed quite tempting, especially since Jones was acting as an expert of the US watch industry.[37]

Regardless of the fact that the early IWC failed in the end, the trends Jones was setting in the late 1860s and early 1870s would be taken up by others who transformed the Swiss watch business completely by the end of the century. The "shock of Philadelphia in 1876"[38] would force watch companies to respond to new challenges and to introduce new production methods. Many followed Jones's path and adopted the American system of watchmaking, while the local authorities supported this technological transformation politically and economically to keep Swiss watch production alive and consequently to protect its global strength and relevant jobs as well. Initially, watch manufacturers in Switzerland had been skeptical about these changes because the complexity of a movement made serial production quite complicated.[39] Furthermore, many considered a watch to be a luxury good that was not supposed to be sold to the masses. Nevertheless, many companies in Switzerland, including the IWC, were able to manage this transition toward industrialized mass production successfully in the last third of the 19th century. What makes the history of the IWC and Jones so special is that the latter attempted this transition early on and would thereby lead the way. It is almost tragic that he did not succeed in the end, and this is why he was forgotten relatively quickly by the watch industry and those unfamiliar with the IWC's history. He faced a lot of problems because he probably thought in much bigger terms than most of his contemporaries and was willing to take risks, something the rather conservative watchmakers of Switzerland were initially not interested in.

Considering the three types of watch production in the 19th century, i.e. single production, serial production, and mass production, Swiss watchmakers did not reach the last of these before the end of the 19th century. Jones, who wanted to be at this point much earlier, faced multiple problems, for example, when he wanted to introduce more models and produce them in larger

---

[37] Seyffer, "Watchmaking," 19.
[38] Ibid.
[39] Karl Marx, *Das Kapital*, vol. 1 (Hamburg: Otto Meissner, 1867), 345.

numbers for an anonymous mass market in the United States.[40] This caused several further problems, especially since the strongly decentralized structures that had existed for a long time could not simply be centralized, and in addition, the knowledge and work skills Jones expected were not uniformly available.[41] The Swiss workers needed to learn how to apply machinery to the production process first. To achieve an output according to the standards of the American system of watchmaking would consequently take much more time than Jones had anticipated, but this issue was tied to the specific context of watch production in Switzerland. The centralization the American watchmaker had in mind was therefore relatively hard to achieve, and it would demand a large amount of capital.[42] He also needed to persuade traditional watchmakers to work with him and investors to provide the necessary financial assets to get the American system of watchmaking installed in his factory. As long as Swiss exports were high, the argument for a transition was hard to make. Similar to other technological developments, e.g. military technology,[43] the trigger for change needed to be a crisis. This crisis actually did occur, but at a time when Jones's attempt was already doomed.

In 1872, the traditional techniques were still solid enough to produce an export value of CHF 18.3 million, an amount that, however, would drop to CHF 13.1 million in 1873 and as low as CHF 4.8 million in 1876.[44]

It is obvious that the Philadelphia Centennial not only caused a psychological shock but also encapsulated the reasons why there was a steady loss in the market share for Swiss-made watches in the United States.[45] With exports of watches declining in the 1870s, Swiss watchmakers realized that a transformation with regard to their method of production was necessary and more than urgent.[46]

---

[40] Seyffer, *Die Unternehmensgeschichte*, 64-65.
[41] In addition, Jones would be confronted with a more confident working class, which had formed during the 19th century in Switzerland as well. See Laurence Marti, *L'émergence du monde ouvrier en Suisse au XIXe siècle* (Neuchâtel: Suisse Editions Livreo-Alphil, 2019).
[42] Seyffer, *Die Unternehmensgeschichte*, 65.
[43] For a detailed discussion of the evolutionary development of military technology, see Frank Jacob and Gilmar Visoni-Alonzo, *The Military Revolution in Early Modern Europe: A Revision* (London: Palgrave Macmillan, 2016).
[44] Seyffer, "Watchmaking," 19.
[45] Ibid., 13.
[46] Edouard Favre-Perret provides a detailed evalutation of the American system of watchmaking by a Swiss representative who had visited the Centennial as a member of the international jury for pocket watches. See Edouard Favre-Perret, *Rapport présenté au haut conseil fédéral sur l'industrie de l'horlogerie: Exposition de Philadelphie, 1876, Section Suisse, Groupe XXV* (Winterthur: Westfehling 1877).

The Centennial counted 10 million visitors and more than 30,000 exhibitors presented their newest products there, including the best machine-made US pocket watches.[47]

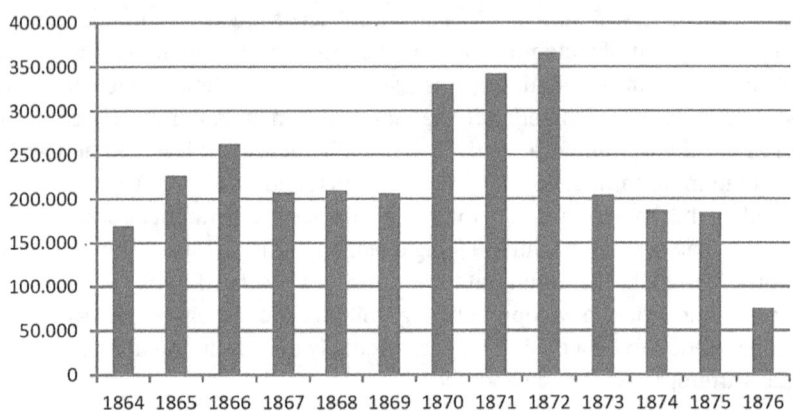

Table 3.1: Swiss watch exports to the United States.[48]

Swiss watchmakers were in danger of being left behind and eventually decided in favor of the transition Jones initially had had in mind when he began to apply the American system of watchmaking in Schaffhausen. Like the American, his Swiss competitors now realized that skills and money were necessary to achieve a fully automated watch production system.[49] With the industrialization of the watch industry in Switzerland during the 1880s and 1890s, an industry to build precise production tools and machines was established as well. Jones, however, the pioneer who had tried to industrialize Swiss watchmaking eight years before the Philadelphia Centennial when he founded his watch company in 1868, had been forgotten by then, and although his legacy still exists, his ideas and innovative thoughts deserve to be honored today as well. Why, however, he chose Schaffhausen as a site for his factory might need some explanation.

Jones's move to the city was quite the opposite to the dominating migration movements of the time. The daily newspaper *Tageblatt für den Kanton Schaffhausen* reported on August 25, 1868 that in the first half of the year, 59

---

[47] *Visitors' Guide to the Centennial Exhibition and Philadelphia* (Philadelphia: J.B. Lippincott & Co., 1876); Thomas Bentley, *The Illustrated Catalogue of the Centennial Exhibition, Philadelphia, 1876* (New York: John Filmer, 1876).
[48] Seyffer, "Innovation oder Nachahmung?" 16.
[49] Seyffer, *Die Unternehmensgeschichte*, 61.

people had left the canton to settle in North America, taking with them capital worth CHF 15,000.[50] Emigration was viewed rather critically, as the region lost not only financial capital but also human capital, and the support from the government for people willing to leave Switzerland was considered to be of ambivalent value.[51] Emigration agents were advertising in the local newspapers,[52] and the region seemed to attract people who were looking for a better future. Jones, on the other hand, considered Schaffhausen to be an ideal place for his watch company. The city had only become economically more important in the second half of the 19th century, and it had not previously been a center of Swiss watchmaking.[53] Maybe Jones chose Schaffhausen because he thought he might easily be able to find investors in a city like that, seeing as people had not yet gained a lot from watchmaking and probably could not disprove his statements that easily either. Jones must have been aware that he needed money and skilled workers, and it would have been harder to get both in a region in which his new watch company had direct competitors for both. All in all, it was probably a mix of factors that made Jones choose Schaffhausen as the place to build his dream.

In 1848, internal tariffs in Switzerland had been abandoned, so it was easier and cheaper to produce and sell within all parts of the country. Four years later, the city of Schaffhausen also abolished the guild system, which made labor contracts much easier in the years afterward. In 1862, economically potent Schaffhausen citizens[54] had founded a union to support industrialization, and in 1873 the Schaffhausener Handelsbank (trade bank) was established. For Jones, these developments were vital, as there seemed to be sufficient support for ventures like his watch company, and the 1870s could be considered as years of industrial opportunities in Schaffhausen.[55] The IWC, from the start, sought to involve the public as investors, as they could buy shares and thereby gain from the company's success as well. Wine trader Gustav Stokar-Egloff (1815-1889) was an important supporter of Schaffhausen's industrialization; he had supported it not only as a leading member of the above-named union but also as a member of the IWC's board of directors.[56]

---

[50] *Tageblatt für den Kanton Schaffhausen*, August 25, 1868.
[51] *Tageblatt für den Kanton Schaffhausen*, September 16, 1868.
[52] See advertisement for P. Becker, Emigration agent, in *Tageblatt für den Kanton Schaffhausen*, January 5, 1871.
[53] Seyffer, *Die Unternehmensgeschichte*, 107.
[54] For a list, see ibid., 108.
[55] Markus Späth-Walter and Historischer Verein des Kantons Schaffhausen, *Schaffhauser Kantonsgeschichte des 19. und 20. Jahrhunderts*, vol. 1 (Schaffhausen: Meier, 2002), 331-340.
[56] Seyffer, *Die Unternehmensgeschichte*, 109.

The building of the Moser Dam in 1866 was also important, as the Schaffhausen waterworks could now provide cheap electrical energy, which was an essential aspect for many of the companies in the city that were founded in the time period following that year. In addition to energy, Jones could also rent rooms he needed for his production process relatively cheaply, and men and women who had been part of the établissage system as home workers could also be recruited there.[57] While the city had had no complete watch production site before Jones founded the IWC in 1868, there had been multiple production sites for parts and cases as well as jewelers before.[58] There had also been attempts to broaden watch production in the city when a watchmaker school was opened in 1856, but this had to be closed four years later due to a lack of students.[59] It is important to emphasize here that Jones could therefore assume that there would be support for his idea of a watch company in Schaffhausen from the city council and investors, as there had been attempts to establish watch production there before. Consequently, one can also argue here that Jones realized that his dream would be attractive for the people of Schaffhausen and that he would be able to sell it to them easily when he started looking for potential investors.

With the right place identified, Jones could eventually begin to realize his dream of a watch company in Switzerland that would produce watches according to American standards. This important story in the globalization of the American system of watchmaking shall now be described in more detail.

3.2. Jones and His Watch Company

Considering the role of Swiss watches on the global market around the 1850s, it is surprising that it should have been an American who first established a watch company in Schaffhausen. Jones had already traveled to Europe in 1867[60] while he was still working for Howard.[61] Whilst there, he would not only travel to Paris for the world's fair[62] but also to Switzerland. Seyffer assumes that Jones used this trip to evaluate the possibilities for setting up his business in a Swiss city and eventually decided on Schaffhausen.[63] The American's impression of Switzerland

---

[57] Ibid., 109-110. On Schaffhausen's watchmaking tradition, see also Schaffhauser "Uhren-Tradition," in *Hundert Jahre IWC: Sonderbeilage 1968 der Schaffhauser Nachrichten*, StdA SH, D III 02.16/03
[58] Seyffer, *Die Unternehmensgeschichte*, 112.
[59] Ibid., 113.
[60] Pass applications F.A. Jones, IWC Archive, DC 04-27.
[61] Seyffer, *Die Unternehmensgeschichte*, 114.
[62] Seyffer, "Watchmaking," 24.
[63] Seyffer, *Die Unternehmensgeschichte*, 121.

must have been positive, as there were sufficient skilled workers who could be hired at a comparatively low cost, considering the wages required for American watchmakers and specialized labor. It is hard to say exactly when and why Jones eventually decided to move to Schaffhausen to establish his own watch company, but his ideas might have been stimulated by talks with Dennison, who was already importing watch parts from Switzerland for the Tremont Watch Company.[64] To what extent the two men talked about Jones's idea is unknown, but it can be assumed that they at least broached the subject.

It would have been impossible for the young American to establish a watch company in his home country for two reasons: 1) Jones would have to find willing investors who, after the Civil War, were rare, as most people interested in the watch trade had already invested in one of the companies that were set up in 1864, and 2) he would have to recruit a skilled workforce, which would also have been scarce due to the demand from competing companies. To sum Jones's problems up, it would simply have been too expensive to found his own watch company in the United States after the Civil War. To save costs and to produce as cheaply as possible, Jones, like many business owners who followed him, decided to outsource production. With regard to this decision, Jones was definitely one of the pioneers in the watch business, and "[c]rossing the Atlantic was a logical but a bold step in those days. For a 27-year-old, the decision was almost foolhardy."[65] Jones would stay in Switzerland until 1876, when he returned to the United States and probably worked as a watch dealer in New York until 1883, but his history as a watch producer was rather short-lived. Nevertheless, in eight years, he had succeeded in installing a fully operational watch production process in Schaffhausen and thereby laid the ground for the International Watch Company's success until today. The watches of the IWC in Schaffhausen therefore still bear an American legacy, and in the early years combined Swiss craftsmanship and the American system of watchmaking to a symbiotic perfection.

That Jones decided to build his dream in Schaffhausen was probably also due to the lack of competition there. There was a tradition of watchmaking in the city, as was outlined in the previous chapter, but the structures in existence were rather related to the production of watch parts and not, like in the centers of watchmaking in Geneva or other parts of Switzerland, the assembling and selling of full watches. Jones had consequently found a gap that offered him the opportunity to build a watch company from scratch that would produce watch movements according to the American system of watchmaking for exportation to the United States. That Schaffhausen had just begun to become a more

---

[64] Seyffer, "Watchmaking," 24.
[65] Ibid., 25.

industrialized business center since the 1850s helped Jones as well, because there was some kind of start-up boom in the city that stimulated investors to take risks with funding new companies. In addition, a route that linked Zurich via Winterthur with Romanshorn was constructed in 1855/56, strengthening the area's logistical infrastructure and the possibilities to connect Schaffhausen to an international market. Ten years later, the Rhine could be used to provide the city with energy. This could have stimulated Jones to decide on the city of Schaffhausen as well, since this was an "epoch-making innovation"[66] and cheap energy was an essential element for a successfully industrialized system of production. Due to this development, Heinrich Moser (1805–1874), who owned the waterworks in Schaffhausen, offered to rent out factory buildings that were connected to energy supplies from water power, something that actually offered a fair amount of convenience for new companies that started their business in Schaffhausen.[67]

Jones had consequently chosen a city in a region whose economic elite wanted to advance, and in Switzerland nothing expressed economic advancement as much as a watch factory. The American watchmaker therefore gained from the enthusiasm and euphoria of investors about his plan and the logistic means to fulfill his own dream. He also could rely on Georg Fischer, a local businessman who traded metal and steel and who already had experience with delivering these to the watch industry of the French part of the Swiss Jura.[68] In the region around Schaffhausen, many local and smaller businesses had been working in the watch trade in Switzerland before, so Jones could easily use these resources for his own business as well. While he had hoped for skilled workers who were cheaper than those in the United States, he could only partly fulfill this hope, as there were home workers who had experience with the manufacturing of watch parts in the region as well, who thus lacked experience with the industrial production of watches Jones had in mind for his factory. It consequently would take some time until everything was ready and

---

[66] Seyffer, Die Unternehmensgeschichte, 116.
[67] Seyffer, "Watchmaking," 26. On the agreement between Moser and the city, see Heinrich Moser, *Die Förderung einheimischer Industrie durch Wasserbauten im Rhein betreffend, zwischen der Stadtgemeinde Schaffhausen einerseits, und Hernn Heinrich Moser auf Charlottenfels, anderseits* (Schaffhausen: Murbach & Dechslin, 1861). On Moser's life and impact, see Adam Pfaff, Heinrich Moser: *Ein Lebensbild* (Schaffhausen: Verlag der Brodtmann'schen Buchhandlung, 1875) and Roger Nicholas Balsiger, *Heinrich Moser (1805–1874): Internationaler Uhrenfabrikant, visionärer Industriepionier* (Zurich: Verein für wirtschaftshistorische Studien, 2007).
[68] Seyffer, *Die Unternehmensgeschichte*, 116.

had achieved the level of production Jones had anticipated and demanded for his venture.

Fig. 3.2.1: Monument to Heinrich Moser in Schaffhausen's "Mosergarten" (Moser garden), photo taken by Hauserphoton, April 4, 2020.[69]

It is not certain exactly when the American watchmaker established his business in Schaffhausen, although numerous sources point to 1868.[70] Seyffer argues that his early activities go back to 1867, and since Jones's residence permit was granted by the city on 1 June 1869,[71] it can be assumed that the young American had started his business operations in Switzerland within this time period. One can therefore only agree with Seyffer's overall evaluation that

---

[69] Accessed December 1, 2020. https://commons.wikimedia.org/wiki/File:Heinrich_uMoser._Schaffhauser_Industriepionier.jpg.

[70] Report of the Invesitgative Commission Weidlich, September 24, 1875, IWC-Archive, DC03-2, 22; Seyffer, *Die Unternehmensgeschichte*, 121-122; Seyffer, "Watchmaking," 28.

[71] Florentine A. Jones, Entry no. 2961, in: Population register, N3, No. 1501-3866, January 28, 1858 until December 8, 1873, StdA SH. Interestingly, the register states 1840 as Jones's birth year, while his birth certificate states 1841. See also "Florentine Ariosto Jones," IWC, June 30, 2015. Accessed December 1, 2020. https://www.iwc.com/de/de/articles/experiences/florentine-ariosto-jones.html.

refers to the period between 1867 and 1869 as the "foundation phase"[72] of Jones's watch business in Schaffhausen. What is also unknown is the role Charles Louis Kidder played. He was born in Palmyra, Ohio in 1836/37, and he and his wife initially accompanied Jones before leaving again in 1872.[73] Kidder was "trained as a specialist in the construction and technology of machinery,"[74] but it is not certain if he was Jones's business partner or just a capable machine worker the latter had recruited to help him install the necessary machinery in Schaffhausen.[75] One aspect that points to Kidder being more than just a worker in the new company is that some of the early movements produced by Jones's factory have Kidder's name engraved on them.[76] Maybe Kidder was sent with Jones by possible US investors to secure support and conduct observations during the early period of the business, but as said before, this must all remain speculation. The only thing that can be said for certain is that Kidder returned to the US in 1872 and later worked for the Cornell Watch Company in Chicago.[77]

Whatever their exact relationship might have been, Jones and Kidder began their business small, and it took some time to prepare a functioning production system.[78] It was not until 1872 that Jones rented additional rooms from the city's central administration to expand his production capacities.[79] At the start, probably in 1869, he had only rented rooms that were offered by Moser on the latter's industrial complex.[80] At the beginning, Jones and Kidder had to train their workers with regard to the demands for an industrial production system that would match the standards of the American system of watchmaking. In addition, the two men must have worked on prototypes for their later production and started to get in contact with other businessmen in Schaffhausen and the region. The extent to which Jones might have referred to his identity as a freemason and member of a lodge in Washington is not known, but since he was initiated in 1868, he might have seen this membership as an entry ticket to the business elite of the Schaffhausen region. It is unclear where Jones got the money from to finance his early activities, however, which makes it unlikely that he was acting totally alone.

---

[72] Seyffer, *Die Unternehmensgeschichte*, 123.
[73] Charles Ludwig Kidder, Entry no. 2962, in: Population register, N3, No. 1501-3866, January 28, 1858 until December 8, 1873, StdA SH.
[74] Seyffer, "Watchmaking," 28.
[75] Tölke and King, *IWC*, 18.
[76] Seyffer, "Watchmaking," 28.
[77] "A Chicago Industry: Description of the Works of the Cornell Watch Company," *Chicago Tribune*, December 13, 1873.
[78] Seyffer, *Die Unternehmensgeschichte*, 123.
[79] Rental contract, September 21, 1872, StdA SH, CII 58.33/001.
[80] Seyffer, *Die Unternehmensgeschichte*, 124.

Seyffer assumes that Jones and Kidder had initially produced watch parts and fittings for watches to generate an income,[81] but all in all the money must have been provided by someone more financially capable than Jones and Kidder. The establishment of a production process that would actually allow mass production was quite cost-intensive, and therefore, a lot of capital was needed in the early years when Jones began to build up his business in Switzerland. According to the latter's own statements, it took four years (until 1872) before the machines and the production process were in place in the way he had anticipated. In late June 1869, Jones eventually registered F. A. Jones & Comp. with the cantonal government,[82] and for the fiscal year 1869/70 the company's total assets amounted to CHF 20,000. Only CHF 142 had to be paid in taxes, emphasizing that Jones and Kidder had not been able to generate a lot of income yet, but the "American watch fabrication," as it was referred to in the Annual Report of the Schaffhausen Waterworks Company, had been in existence and rented production sites from the latter. The company's costs therefore surmounted its income, and without any investment from unknown parties, the business could hardly have stayed alive. The fact that Jones had frequently traveled back and forth to the United States in this early period leads to the assumption that he had more than likely been financed by some American investors.[83]

Jones never clearly communicated with his Swiss investors about his finances, and it was probably similar with Kidder, who was not probably not involved in the financial aspects of the company. Whatever the reason was, Jones and Kidder separated in 1871/72, and the latter went back to the United States with his wife. The former changed the entry and name for his watch company to F. A. Jones on 1 June 1871, and in the following years the machines eventually worked sufficiently well that the production of watches could actually start.[84] Like the American watch companies that had been founded in 1864, Jones had to survive the initial, capital-intensive period to set up the machinery and train the workers in the skills needed to start producing quality watches. That he managed to reach the production period is marvelous, but at the same time poses a lot of questions. In particular, the questions related to the acquisition of capital makes it quite unlikely to consider the whole venture to be a one-man show. However, without new and so far unknown sources, it is up to the reader to decide if the story of a daring individual can be upheld.

---

[81] Ibid.
[82] Ragionenbuch Kanton Schaffhausen, vol. 11, Entry No. 278, S.554, State Archive Kanton Schaffhausen (STASH), cited in ibid., 123.
[83] Seyffer, "Watchmaking," 28.
[84] Ibid.

From the start, Jones had planned to produce watch movements in Switzerland and sell them in the United States, once they had been put into cases. What is interesting, yet must also remain speculation here, is the fact that Dennison produced watchcases in England and exported them. So maybe there was an overall plan to combine watches and cases produced abroad to be sold by an American company, like the one by Eugene Paulus mentioned before. However, this is a rather speculative consideration, but it would also speak for a larger network of investors and people involved that would have had an interest in Jones's success in Switzerland. What nevertheless speaks for a network of American investors is the fact that there existed two joint-stock companies in relation to Jones's company, one in Switzerland and a parallel one in New York City, where, according to a catalog from 1873, the principal office of the company was located, namely in Maiden Lane, the main artery of the watch and jewelers' businesses.[85] To advertise his watches on the American market, Jones would also use the image of a factory building, which actually did not exist yet, but thereby matched the marketing strategies of other watch producers in the United States.[86]

The International Watch Company was so named as these parallel Swiss and American joint-stock companies were founded in August 1871 and Jones had recruited investors for this venture on both sides of the Atlantic.[87] How the American was able to raise capital was always part of the mysterious aura surrounding Jones,[88] but in April 1871 he was able to get Hiram W. Smith and James B. Brown, both active in the areas of American watch production and trade, involved to establish the International Watch Company in New York. The shared capital was US$ 100,000, equating to CHF 500,000 at the time, and Schaffhausen was considered a branch of this corporation that had been set up under US law.[89] At the same time, he set up a Swiss company on trial with the name International Watch Company together with the investors and shareholders Edouard and Ali Berthoulet from Les Ponts-de-Martel, Switzerland and Robert C. Neher from the Schweizerische Industrie Gesellschaft (Swiss Industry Company).[90] This second joint-stock company was founded according to Swiss law, and a contract divided the company's worth of CHF 60,000 into 24 shares, valued at CHF 2,500 each. Of

---

[85] Seyffer, *Die Unternehmensgeschichte*, 125.
[86] *The Jewelers Circular and Horological Review* 5, no. 4, May 15, 1874: 1-2.
[87] Founding Contract IWC, Les Ponts-de-Martel, August 1, 1871, STASH, RRRA 2/7297.
[88] Michael Friedberg, "F. A. Jones: The Man and the Mystery." Accessed December 1, 2020. https://www.iwc.com/ch/en/forum/the-man-and-the-mystery.html.
[89] Seyffer, *Die Unternehmensgeschichte*, 126; Seyffer, "Watchmaking," 29.
[90] Theo Keller, *Schweizerische Industrie-Gesellschaft, Neuhausen am Rheinfall, 1853-1953* (Neuhausen am Rheinfall: SIG, 1953).

these shares, Jones held 8, Neher 10, and the Berthoulet brothers 3 each. The contract for the establishment of the joint-stock company also listed all business assets, which, in 1871, including all movable goods and patents, amounted to CHF 322,500.[91]

Between August 1871 and July 1872, consequently, "the American corporation with its head office in New York and the Schaffhausen company on trial under Swiss law existed side by side, with different shareholders but under the same name of International Watch Company."[92] In the summer of 1872, however, Jones took over all shares of the company in New York when his cooperation with Smith ended. Jones appointed John A. Dawson, with whom he had worked at Howard's watch company before, as a new director on the US side. Considering how many other American watchmakers and investors were involved during that period, it is hard to believe that Jones was really up for a one-man show in Switzerland; it seems far more likely that the plan for a Swiss watch company had been sanctioned by a group of US investors early on. Otherwise, it is doubtful why men familiar with the trade would have supported someone like Jones. There might nevertheless have also been a practical reason to establish both an American and a Swiss company, namely to circumvent import tolls.[93]

To be successful, Jones needed to sell his watches to the United States as cheaply as possible, and this seems to have been a possibility. Later, F. H. Mathez would become the general agent for the IWC in the US in 1873[94] before the American joint-stock company was sold by Brown and Dawson for CHF 800,000.[95] CHF 450,000 had to be paid in cash and the rest in shares, and with the New York IWC ceasing to exist, Schaffhausen became the headquarters and remained the only IWC. In 1874, a joint-stock company was established and demanding that investors sign up for shares in it. In the meantime, Jones had been able to get production running, although he would not receive payment for his watches as they were to be paid relatively late, namely 90 days after shipping. That meant that Jones needed to wait for an inflow of capital for produced watches for three months, a fact that quite substantially weakened his financial capacities.[96]

Nevertheless, in 1872, Jones was eventually able to begin serial production of his first calibres, usually referred to as "Jones calibres." The production

---

[91] Seyffer, *Die Unternehmensgeschichte*, 126.
[92] König, "The International Watch Company," 31.
[93] Seyffer, *Die Unternehmensgeschichte*, 127.
[94] An advertisement can be found in *The Watchmaker and Jeweller*, May 1873.
[95] Seyffer, *Die Unternehmensgeschichte*, 127-128.
[96] König, "The International Watch Company," 31.

numbers rose and Jones needed more rooms, so he rented, as mentioned above, some additional rooms in the city. Within one and a half years, Jones had been able to finish 6,000 watches for sale and, in addition, parts for around 5,000 movements. After 4-5 years, he was finally at a point where he was producing watches quite fast and could make money by selling them.[97] Jones produced a variety of watches, and according to König, "[d]uring that period, he must have designed the *ébauche* family known today as C/S/R/D with the new common train."[98]

Fig. 3.2.2: A "Jones calibre," raw movement, serial no. 16688.

Initially, Jones had also produced movements of an older generation, but with his own calibres (C/S/R/D), he proved that he was able to provide his own product line.[99] These were named Romney, Greenleaf, Craig, Bradley and Burns, presumably after his grandmother Permelia Craig or his uncle Dennis H. Craig, his own brother, etc. All in all, however, the first production period from the end of the experiments until the foundation of the joint-stock company in 1874 is relatively poorly documented. Nevertheless, König guesses that "the period from August 1872 to January 1874 was probably the most pleasant time that F. A. Jones experiences in Schaffhausen."[100] He was quite successful, and he was still the only proprietor of his factory. He had not only

---

[97] Ibid., 33; Seyffer, *Die Unternehmensgeschichte*, 129.
[98] König, "The International Watch Company," 33.
[99] König, "The International Watch Company," 33.
[100] Ibid., 31.

produced watch movements but also started his own product line that shared a basic design drafted by Jones, and his production worked well according to a more standardized as well as mechanical process. It is therefore important to highlight that Jones had already succeeded in implementing the American system of watchmaking in Schaffhausen by the end of 1873, making him one of the pioneers of modern watch production in Switzerland.[101]

Table 3.2.1: Types of Jones's ébauches.[102]

Type of ébauche	Pattern	Ligne	Type	Material	Jewels
1N	B	19	early key wind, key set	nickel/brass	11-16
2N	H/E	19	early stem wind, lever set, hunter, 43.3 mm three-quarter bridge	nickel	16-20
3N	B	19	stem-wind, stem-set, hunter	nickel/brass	11-16
4N	S/R/D	19	common train, stem-wind, stem-set, hunter	nickel	11-16
5N	C/S/R	19	common train, key-wind, key-set	nickel/brass	11-15
6N	B/S/R/D/H/E	19	stem-wind, stem-set, Lépine	nickel/brass	11-16
7N	H/E	19	late stem-wind, lever set, hunter, 43.7 mm three-quarter bridge	nickel	16-20
8N	B/R	15	hunter	nickel	11-15?
9N	B/S/R/H	16	unknown	unknown	unknown

Technologically, Jones and his company were more than up-to-date and were forerunners of a general trend that would be broadly applied in the late 19th century. Regardless of these successes, the young American entrepreneur needed money. His further plans demanded a factory building to further centralize the production process, and, for the moment, he also needed to cover the problem of a lack of capital, since most of his sales would, as mentioned before, only be paid 90 days after shipment. Jones, due to tolls and

---

[101] Ibid., 34.
[102] Alan Myers, "Construction and Development of the F.A. Jones Watch," in David Seyffer, Thomas König and Alan Myers, *F. A. Jones: His Life, Legacy and Watches* (Schaffhausen: IWC, 2013), 67.

export costs, probably also never intended to produce a massive number of complete watches but would rather only export the movements, which would be put into cases and finished by US jewelers. The first catalog from 1872/73 consequently only contained the different movements Jones was able to offer at that time, showing that Jones had fully believed in a total division of watch production. What is interesting, though, is that his movements were not meant to fit the standard US case, which is why he needed somebody—he might have thought of Dennison—who could provide him with the necessary watch cases to finish the watches and get them ready for sale.[103] The extent to which Jones already had ties to people in the trade who could provide him with special cases for his own watch portfolio is unknown, but Jones had begun to sell watches and therefore someone must have produced suitable watch cases as well.

While it was relatively easy with regard to the US watch and jewelers trade to sell a small number of no-name products, Jones wanted to sell his watches under the IWC label as well and therefore worked with Mathez, as a general sales agent, to get his brand known on the other side of the Atlantic as fast as possible. He had been able to set up a mass production system, and now Jones needed customers. Contacts with US wholesalers were therefore important, and the IWC was consequently a transnational venture from the moment the first watches left the company. When Mathez tried to trigger sales, Jones's watches were advertised as a hybrid of the American system of watchmaking and skilled Swiss labor.[104] König, referencing Charles S. Crossman's work from 1886,[105] highlights with regard to Jones's successful marketing that he "became somewhat of a celebrity in connection with the International Watch Company … who tried to make watches with machinery built in America."[106] In spring 1873, sales nevertheless began in the United States, and Jones seemed to have made his dream a reality. Dawson, with whom Jones shared a past at Howard's watch company, would supposedly also have used his contacts in the watch trade to trigger the interest of possible buyers in the IWC's products. The former assistant superintendent, who had worked for a well-known watch company in the United States, "was thus the perfect missionary who, as [a] recognized expert with superior knowledge, could explain to the small local watchmaker or jeweller the advantages of quality watches in general and of IWC in particular."[107]

---

[103] Ibid., 35.
[104] Ibid., 36.
[105] Crossman, *Complete History*.
[106] König, "The International Watch Company," 37.
[107] Ibid., 37.

Table 3.2.2: Estimated number of Jones's movements that were marketed until 1878.[108]

Pattern	Type	Estimated Number Marketed
19 ligne - B	key-wind	1,700
	stem-wind hunter	3,500
	stem-wind Lépine	400
19 ligne - H	stem-wind hunter	2,500
	stem-wind Lépine	150
19 ligne - E	stem-wind hunter	700
	stem-wind Lépine	20
19 ligne - C	key-wind	2,000
	key-wind	1,000
19 ligne - R	key-wind	200
	stem-wind hunter	5,000
	stem-wind Lépine	1,000
19 ligne - S	key-wind	100
	stem-wind hunter	5,000
	stem-wind Lépine	1,000
19 ligne - D	stem-wind hunter	900
	stem-wind Lépine	200
15 ligne - B/R	stem-wind hunter	100
16 ligne - B/S/R/H	unknown	1,500

In fact, the perception of the IWC was not bad, and Jones could be happy with his achievements and his sales numbers, which were quite good. In his time at the IWC, he sold ca. 15,000 watch movements to the United States—he had produced around 18,700 raw movements while he had been in Schaffhausen,

---

[108] Ibid., 63.

close to 7,000 alone in 1876/77, the year he left—and they were also technologically innovative.[109]

Fig. 3.2.3: Jones calibre pocket watch, Pattern B, key-wind, ca. 1872.

By the end of January 1874, Jones was selling 6,000 movements to the United States and had thereby proven that his idea could actually work out quite well. The work with working boxes and machinery made it possible to produce larger numbers of watch movements relatively fast. Myers describes the functionality and the advantage of the working boxes as follows: "The boxes have 10 main compartments for the plates and auxiliary parts, indicating that Jones watches were manufactured in batches of 10. The bottom plate, three-quarter bridge and balance cock are all engraved with the serial number but some smaller parts, e.g. the pallet bridge, had a number 1 to 10 indicating the movement in the box with which they belong."[110] Jones had consequently established a well-functioning production process and now only needed more capital to continue the success of the IWC.

---

[109] Myers, "Construction and Development," 63-66.
[110] Ibid., 66.

Fig. 3.2.4: Working box used to assemble watches in Jones's factory. IWC Archive, P07-1259.

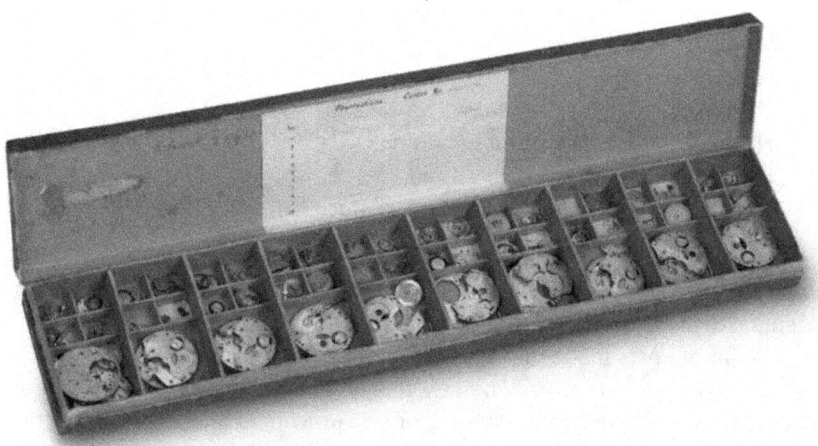

In 1874, a call for possible investors who were interested in buying shares for the IWC was published, in which Jones referred to himself as a former director of E. Howard Watch &. Clock Co., probably to leave no doubt that he still intended to be in charge of his company, regardless of the capital he wanted to gather.[111] The new joint-stock company was actually quite attractive for investors. Not only had Jones established a portfolio of five different types of men's watches, but his company now employed 40 men and 53 women. These employees "manufactured by mechanized production plates, bridges and cocks while the manufacture and fitting of moving parts, especially the escapement, was mostly carried out by small, specialized firms in the Swiss Jura. Due to the employment of such subcontractors, the total number of people working for IWC was, even at this time, significantly higher."[112] Jones wanted to continue his centralization attempt and bring more of this work to Schaffhausen, where he intended to use some of the capital that was supposed to be raised by the establishment of the joint-stock company to erect a company building in the city. However, the initial training of the new workforce also took time, which is why costs increased but production rates stagnated in 1874.

---

[111] IWC-Archive, DC01-1002. On Jones's actual role at Howard's company, see also Gerrit Nijssen, "E. Howard & Company," *Bulletin of the NAWCC* 36, no. 292 (1994): 563-593.
[112] König, "The International Watch Company," 38.

Regardless of these problems, Jones was able to sell the shares, which would bring in close to CHF 1,000,000 of fresh capital that would cover the following costs:

> CHF 610,000 for machines,
> CHF 140,000 for 5,000 watches in production,
> CHF 100,000 for a new factory building,
> CHF 100,000 as working capital, and
> CHF 40,000 for raw materials and other stock.[113]

Jones had also been in contact with Schwob-Frères at La Chaux-de-Fonds, who would sell IWC watches to the Canadian market, so it is clear that he intended to use the new influx of capital to expand to other markets as well. His calculation of costs for the investors was therefore based on the assumption that the IWC would produce and sell 10,000 watches per year. The investors reacted quite euphorically, but their euphoria prevented them from seeing that Jones's calculations were quite finely balanced and that the promised success could only be delivered if no factor in his calculations changed.[114]

The "move to the new tailor-made factory building at No. 15 Baumgarstenstrasse in the first quarter of 1875"[115] would allow Jones to centralize his production, and he "gradually replaced outsourced production by increasing the number of items produced in-house."[116] The bankruptcy-related inventory list of 1876 shows that Jones was able to continue production until late 1875,[117] but the lack of capital and problems with exporting would soon destroy the dream of the young American. Although, as Seyffer correctly emphasizes, "Jones was the first to manufacture high-quality watches under this modern system, based chiefly on the efficient organization of labour and the employment of advanced machine-tool technology" and regardless of the fact that the "IWC had achieved the performance desired by ... Jones,"[118] the company would suffer from similar problems as its American competitors. Some of these problems were related to the international market, others to Jones's personality, and they shall all now be described in some more detail.

---

[113] Ibid., 38-39.
[114] Ibid., 40.
[115] Seyffer, "Watchmaking," 28.
[116] Ibid., 29.
[117] Ibid.
[118] Ibid.

Fig. 3.2.5: IWC pocket watch for women. Only three of them are known to remain worldwide.

Fig. 3.2.6: IWC pocket watch for women. Only three of them are known to remain worldwide.

3.3. Home Made and Global Problems

Financial liquidity had always been Jones's biggest problem in Switzerland, and in this regard the early history of the IWC is no different from those of the American watch companies that were established due to the Civil War boom. In 1873, the Bank of Winterthur requested that Jones should pay his debts immediately, a fact that might have stimulated Jones's decision to ask for further investment with his public announcement to sell shares in the new joint-stock company in 1874. The American had been probably too brisk when he had asked the bank to grant him more money and stretched the time frame to pay it back. He was maybe also frustrated that the bank would not consider his previous achievements and actually demanded more security for further loans than his word and experience. At the end of 1873, Jones had proven by his previous work that a production rate of around 10,000 watches per year was in reach, and he even hoped to increase this number to 15,000. At the same time, he intended to replace the home workers whom the IWC still hired for parts production once the new factory had been built and the local workforce had been recruited and trained.[119]

Jones, regardless of his achievements by the end of 1873, continued to dream big, but he absolutely needed more fresh capital to keep his dream alive. To fulfill his vision of a watch company that would achieve a fully industrial system of production according to the American watchmaking system, the young American could not continue without the support of Swiss investors. The joint-stock company in the United States had not been able to provide sufficient funding for his future plans, which is why Jones began to get in contact with people in Schaffhausen, assisted by businessman Robert Neher, who introduced him to the financial elites of the town and region.[120] In late 1873, a group of interested investors had formed, including Gustav Stokar-Egloff (1815-1889), former president of the Schaffhausen Tradebank (Schaffhauser Handelsbank), the lawyer Hermann Freuler-Ziegler, the physicist Professor Jakob Amsler-Laffon (1823-1912), Heinrich Moser's son Henri (1844-1923), and Julien Rauss, who would later become Jones's assistant at the IWC.[121] Together they founded a joint-stock company, the International Watch Company AG, Schaffhausen (1874-1876), which absorbed the New York branch, and published an announcement that said that interested people could buy company shares.[122] The local daily, the *Tageblatt für den Kanton Schaffhausen*, published an announcement on 14 February 1874 that said that 50 shares could be bought for CHF 1,000 each. It was also reported that the watch company was an important business for the city and that the danger of it moving to Winterthur or any other Swiss city had been prevented by the group of investors that had formed to keep the International

---

[119] König, "The International Watch Company," 41.
[120] Seyffer, *Die Unternehmensgeschichte*, 130.
[121] On Schaffhausen's financial elites and their network, see Adrian Knoepfli, "Eine Schaffhauser Gründung im Allgäu: Die Baumwollspinnerei Wangen (1859-1992)," *Schaffhauser Beiträge* 78 (2004): 239-298, especially 251-253.
[122] Public announcement by the International Watch Company AG, IWC Archive, DC01-1002.

Watch Company in Schaffhausen.[123] Jones had consequently been successful in selling his dream to the people of the Swiss city as well, who feared to lose a business that could soon provide high returns on capital.

Therefore, Stokar-Egloff, Freuler-Ziegler, and Henri Moser had also signed the announcement to make it more trustworthy for possible investors.[124] The latter were promised a return of 10,66%, and a profitability calculation was also provided. This simply seemed to be good to be true and, as it would turn out, Jones had doctored the numbers quite a bit to make them more attractive. The promise of high returns was probably the biggest mistake Jones had made because, due to homemade and external problems, he would be unable to keep these promises.[125] Jones had become the sole proprietor of the New York IWC when Brown and Dawson approved this reorganization on 19 March 1874. In comparison to his American business partners, Jones would face more problems with investors in Switzerland. However, he was able to raise the money necessary to continue his venture for a while before it would eventually go bankrupt in early 1876. Regardless of the fresh money for his plans that would be spent on new machines and the new factory building, among other things, Jones had kept the debts for watches already shipped in the name of IWC in New York when the company was fused with the new IWC AG that would financially not leave him a lot of room for his new endeavors.[126] In addition, Jones had omitted the fact that he owed money to the Bank of Winterthur, which meant that a considerable amount of the new capital would be used to cover the bank's demands for Jones to repay his older loans.[127] All in all, Jones did not tell the truth, or at least left out some important facts so as not to frighten away possible investors.

In February 1874, he was nevertheless able to get another loan from the bank in Schaffhausen, which Jones used to pay his debts with the bank in Winterthur. However, the new board of the joint-stock company had to provide collateral for this financial transaction. The bank in Schaffhausen had also signed up for 25 shares in the new joint-stock company, and therefore had a vital interest in the IWC's further success. With such a close interweaving of financial interests with the future of Jones's watch company, the latter could initially feel quite secure. Considering the new loans and the fresh capital that was gathered, "the financial position of the company looked excellent in early 1874."[128] However, the new board members of the joint-stock company soon began to question

---

[123] *Tageblatt für den Kanton Schaffhausen*, February 14, 1874.
[124] Seyffer, *Die Unternehmensgeschichte*, 131.
[125] Ibid., 145.
[126] König, "The International Watch Company," 42.
[127] Seyffer, *Die Unternehmensgeschichte*, 132.
[128] König, "The International Watch Company," 43.

Jones's uncontested position. They demanded to name the chef de bureau, maybe equivalent to a modern executive director, who would support but also control Jones and his operations on behalf of the board. Jones refused this demand and was unwilling to tolerate any control from the board members over his business, a decision that naturally embittered the relationship between the two parties from the start. In the end, the new board was unwilling to force Jones too far, even though they had demanded a separation of the powers within the company and a better balance between Jones and the investors, as their interest was at stake now, too.

Jones, on the other hand, did not feel the need to include others' interests in his plans and had threatened multiple times to move his production to another Swiss city, maybe Winterthur, a statement that frightened both the city's authorities and the new investors alike. Not only did the bank in Schaffhausen give in when Jones demanded more money, but the Schaffhausen waterworks also granted him cheap land, where he would eventually build his new factory, at Baumgartenstraße 15.[129]

Jones's idea for the new factory building was an imitation of well-known American ones, like Waltham's American Watch Company and others. For such a building project, however, Jones's funds, as outlined for the use of the joint-stock company's capital, was calculated with narrow margins, especially since "[t]he speed with which the plans and offers for land, building and energy supply were tabled, suggests that F.A. Jones wanted to build on a larger scale right from the start, even though a sum of only 100,000 Swiss francs for the construction of the new factory had been put in the financial prospectus, in order not to frighten off investors."[130] Jones had requested not only buying additional property from the waterworks but also additional hydroelectric power—5 horsepower—from the Rhine. This already shows that he not only planned to continue the IWC's watch production in Schaffhausen but also intended to increase the output of watch movements in the near future. Initially, Jones had calculated costs of CHF 10,000 for the property, CHF 20,000 for a new steam engine and boiler house as the necessary hydroelectric power was unavailable, and only CHF 70,000 for the factory building. The latter, however, would eventually cost CHF 120,000, and this was not the only problem. Furthermore, the architect of the factory building, a man named Meyer from Zurich, died before it was finished, and he was replaced by Heinrich Ulrich, an architect who had already been working in Schaffhausen.[131] The costs

---

[129] Projektskizze fer neuen Uhrenfabrik, 1874, StdA SH, Bildersammlung, Strassen A-Z, 13/40.
[130] König, "The International Watch Company," 44. On the building process, see Seyffer, *Die Unternehmensgeschichte*, 134-135.
[131] König, "The International Watch Company," 44.

eventually increased to a sum that was far beyond Jones's original calculation, and this was not the only problem the American had to face in 1874.

Fig. 3.3.1: Half-page IWC advertisement in *The Watchmaker and Jeweller*, May 1873, P06_1893, IWC Archive.

THE

International Watch Co.

with the object of combining all the excellence of the American system of mechanism with the more skilful hand labor of the Swiss, we have established our

Watch Factory at Schaffusen,

SWITZERLAND,

and are now prepared to furnish to the TRADE reliable time keeping watches, having all the advantages of absolute mechanical perfection, and art'sti finish. We make a specialty of stem winding and stem-setting movements, and guarantee them to be not only the least liable to get out of order, but to be in every respect as durable as key-winders.

Our line of Watches, of seventeen different patterns, possess all the requisites of accurate time-keepers, and can be sold at prices which defy competition.

For descriptive catalogue, &c., apply to

F. H. MATHEZ, General Agent,

No. 5 Maiden Lane, New York.

The originally requested hydroelectric power was not available because a pier that was under construction had collapsed into the Rhine in August. As a consequence, Jones had to buy a steam engine that was much more expensive than expected, as it, in combination with a boiler house, cost him CHF 43,000.[132] Jones was therefore short on money again, although at least the factory building was ready to move into in early 1875. Regardless of this success, production output had decreased due to these multiple problems, which also worsened the relationship between Jones and his investors. While the American watchmaker had kept a lot of financial aspects hidden from the latter, he had also changed the product portfolio in this financially stressful time without any consultation with the board. In 1872, as described in the last chapter, Jones had produced seven types of watches, based on two basic types of raw movements (B/H), and when he presented the costs for the near future to the investors in early 1874, he omitted the fact that he intended to broaden the portfolio to keep up with the demands of the market. At the same time, he had not accurately calculated the costs for the development and production of new models when presenting his business plan. The investors could consequently not have realized when signing up for shares that the developmental period of the IWC was not fully concluded.[133] This would of course arouse the anger of those under financial pressure, and Jones would soon be confronted with some more heat, especially since the American market also caused trouble due to a decline in possible sales.

Due to the Panic of 1873,[134] the US market for watches faced a crisis as well. The demand for watches dropped abruptly; Elgin had to stop production for nine months and imports from Switzerland also decreased in numbers, a development that made the investors in Schaffhausen quite nervous. In the United States, as a consequence of the economic crisis, Elgin and Waltham, i.e. the biggest watch companies, began a ruthless price war for the American market, and Robbins & Appleton, the owners of Waltham, decided to produce their own cases to save costs as well. *The Jewelers' Circular and Horological Review* reported the following about the "American Watch Cases" in January 1875:

> It seems to be a peculiarly American fashion in business to concentrate under one system the entire work of production, from the crudest

---

[132] Ibid.; Seyffer, *Die Unternehmensgeschichte*, 135.
[133] König, "The International Watch Company," 45-46.
[134] Nicolas Barreyre, "The Politics of Economic Crises: The Panic of 1873, the End of Reconstruction, and the Realignment of American Politics," *Journal of the Gilded Age and Progressive Era* 10, no. 4 (2011): 403-423; Hannah Catherine Davies, *Transatlantic Speculations: Globalization and the Panics of 1873* (New York: Columbia University Press, 2018).

materials to the perfect product of the nicest manufacturing processes. Indeed, probably no other establishment in the world can boast what is not to be seen in connection with the American Watch Company's ... business, in which the ore is mined from Virginia, and transmuted through the many processes of extracting the metal and making the gold into cases for the American [i.e. Waltham] watches, without the intervention of a single dealer of the payment of a single commission.[135]

This marked a watershed, as the system as it existed before collapsed. Now, watches were completely produced and sold by one of the biggest US companies to retailers, who did not need to buy watch movements and cases separately anymore but bought and sold finished watches instead.[136] In an instant, it seemed, Jones's business model had been abandoned in his main market, a development that would cause serious trouble for him when he could no longer export his product to the United States.

Fig. 3.3.2: Schwob Frères advertisement in *The Jewelers' Circular and Horological Review* 5, no. 10, November 16, 1874: 169.

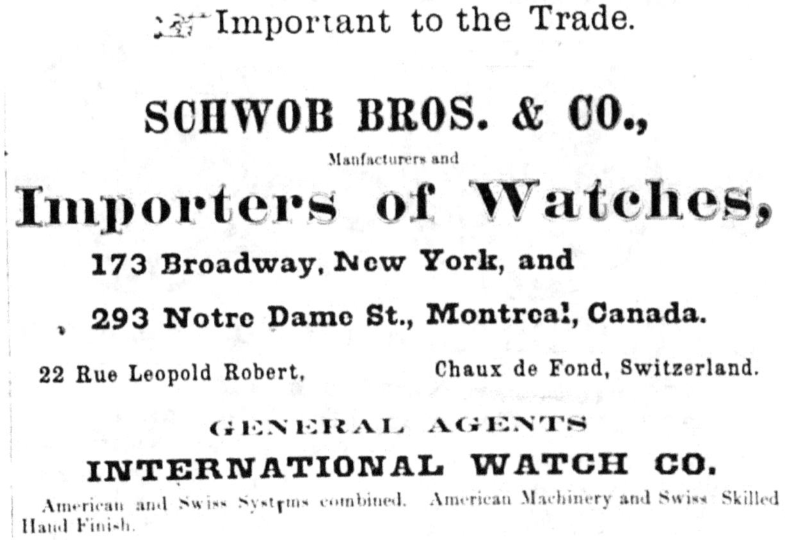

Important to the Trade.

SCHWOB BROS. & CO.,

Manufacturers and

Importers of Watches,

173 Broadway, New York, and

293 Notre Dame St., Montreal, Canada.

22 Rue Leopold Robert,   Chaux de Fond, Switzerland.

GENERAL AGENTS

INTERNATIONAL WATCH CO.

American and Swiss Systems combined. American Machinery and Swiss Skilled Hand Finish.

Smaller businesses were pushed out of the market, and when Elgin went as far as selling watches below production costs to get rid of competitors, the

---

[135] "American Watch Cases," *The Jewelers' Circular and Horological Review* 5, no. 12, January 15, 1875: 208.
[136] König, "The International Watch Company," 47.

American watch trade faced a serious crisis. The imports of Swiss watches rapidly declined from 366,000 in 1872 to only 75,000 in 1876. The IWC did not stand a chance against such price drops, and Jones was now facing a serious issue because his company "was unable to counter this price pressure either by adopting Elgin's price-cutting strategy or by selling complete, fully fitted watches, as Waltham was doing."[137] In June 1874, Jones wanted to establish a sales company with partners in the US to circumvent tolls and to sell his products without too many retailers in between and in August announced to the board that he had signed a two-year contract with Schwob Frères, who would buy the IWC's entire production output. Jones, in return, had agreed to produce a yearly minimum of 9,000 units.[138] This deal also secured him an uninsured loan of CHF 75,000 from the Schaffhausen Tradebank, which meant that he could breathe for a moment again.

Fig. 3.3.3: Schwob Frères advertisement in *The Jewelers' Circular and Horological Review* 6, no. 1, February 1875: 7.

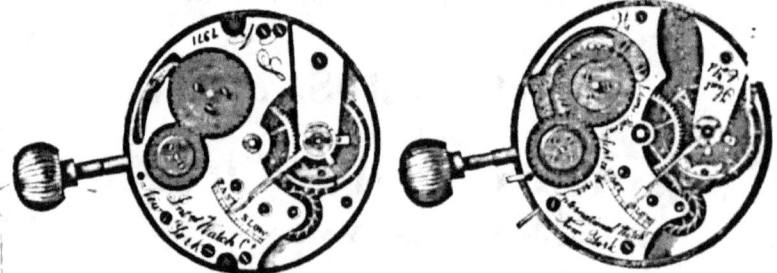

---

[137] Ibid., 49.
[138] Ibid., 50.

Regardless of this deal, Jones also never clearly communicated with his shareholders about the fact that he had not yet completely industrialized his production but was still dependent on homeworkers in Western Switzerland. And not all adopted the new methods of production so easily. Jones consequently had not fully applied mechanized processes yet, and when he pressed his home workers too hard to move to the factory for a centralized production in the winter of 1874/75, they refused to deliver the parts he desperately needed to finish the IWC movements at all. This cut production numbers in a six-week period from 1,500 watches to 41.[139] Furthermore, the move to the new factory building had also decreased the company's output to 300 watches per month between November 1874 and March 1875 with an extreme low of 168 watches in January 1875, and due to the lack of parts there were many unfinished movements in the warehouse. The board demanded an explanation, and Jones now had to address the issue.[140]

As if he were not already in trouble, there were "considerable problems" with the watches delivered to Schwob Frères, namely "with the coating of bottom plates and three-quarter bridges."[141] Jones's business partner in North America claimed that 1,820 movements of the first 8,733 delivered had "suffered from dislocation."[142] Regardless of this problem, Schwob Frères had praised Jones's watches in March 1875, and when the latter had a meeting with the Handelsbank in April, a representative of the former was also present. There it was announced that Schwob Frères "was unable to fulfill the contract due to sales problems but at best could continue to sell watches for IWC on a commission basis."[143] While they had been strong in Canada, Schwob Frères could only offer a small sales office in New York, and with the problems on the US market, they were unable to sell large numbers for the time being, although, as König argued, they would probably have continued to buy 9,000 watches per year if Jones could have provided them.[144] Regardless of this trend, Jones had increased his portfolio to 28 watch models, which he mentioned in his report to the board in June 1875.

The board members, in the meantime, had been skeptical about why Jones had invited a representative of Schwob Frères to the board meeting in March and the bank meeting in April and assumed that he had some kind of financial interest with the Canadian wholesaler. Since Jones had not provided full insight

---

[139] Ibid., 45.
[140] Ibid., 51.
[141] Ibid., 52.
[142] Ibid.
[143] Ibid.
[144] Ibid.

into the actual numbers and conditions at the IWC, the board became more and more suspicious. However, Jones ran out of money, a fact that could not be changed by another CHF 75,000 from the Handelsbank and an unapproved loan by the Banque D'Epargne des Montagnes.[145] Due to decisions that Jones took without first consulting the board, the trench between the two parties intensified, and although communication had already reached its nadir from November 1874 to February 1875, the way the American treated the board in the spring of 1875 damaged whatever trust and hope may have been left. Jones always presented a fait accompli, if he presented anything to the board at all.[146] He might have been successful in establishing the American system of watchmaking at the IWC, and his box system allowed him to react to the demands and necessities of the market, but the Panic of 1873 and the way he treated the board and thereby the investors in Schaffhausen caused external and internal problems that would eventually break his neck. He was later criticized for having calculated everything so tightly that even the smallest issue would have caused a collapse, but it is just as important to acknowledge that his behavior toward the board limited his financial flexibility in the end even more than his technical problems. Jones led the business like an autocrat, refused to speak German, addressing the board in English or French, and considered the investors only responsible for providing money. He was too stubborn to accept advice or to listen to criticism.[147] The technological visionary was eventually not a good businessman, a combination that has driven many inventors into ruin both before and after Jones. The young American insisted on his own dream, and any proposal for change was considered an attack on him. This aspect speaks for the assumption that Jones acted alone, because an American network backing him would probably have interfered at this point, although Jones might have already cut these ties in 1874, but this remains rather speculative.

Before bankruptcy would end Jones's dream, the board again tried to gain some influence in the management of the IWC, and some banks, in such an event, would have been willing to support the company with fresh loans, but they were also demanding some more influence to secure their investment.[148] Jones was not willing to accept such a solution and continued his stubborn course that would determine the year 1875. When CHF 300,000 of debts were displayed at a meeting in May, the board demanded "energetic measures"[149] to

---

[145] Ibid., 53.
[146] Seyffer, *Die Unternehmensgeschichte*, 137.
[147] Ibid., 144-145.
[148] König, "The International Watch Company," 43.
[149] Ibid., 55.

solve the financial problems. Jones, however, was not willing to make any concessions, and the issue was postponed for the moment. The investors felt betrayed in many ways, probably particularly in relation to the costs for the factory building, which in contrast to the estimated CHF 100,000 for property, building, and energy supplies had cost more than twice as much. Soon debts rose to CHF 400,000, and there seemed no way to generate new assets, neither through loans nor through bonds. At the same time, Jones was not even close to producing the promised 10,000 watches per year, and regression claims were made by the first investors.[150]

In his business report from 30 June 1875, Jones tried to explain the situation. The delays with the factory building, the time required to train the workers, an increase in demand for workforces in general, and the demand for capital for further portfolio development and to buy production-related materials had caused the problems the IWC had to face at that point.[151] On 21 August 1875, there was another board meeting, and in absentia Jones demanded the dissolution of the advisory board, whose members nevertheless decided to publish Jones's business report with a critical preface.[152] The dispute was consequently continued in public and Jones published a reply as well.[153] In it, he accused the board of sabotaging his innovative development and thereby the success of the IWC. He admitted that

> I resolutely resisted transferring this right [regarding personnel] into hands who, out of imaginary complaints, could say goodbye to an employee who, with his experience, could not be replaced, at least not before the lapse of several years, which would cause heavy losses to the company. Such large and important responsibilities should never be entrusted to hands who are so little interested in the company.[154]

At the same time, Jones again emphasized the value of his company to Schaffhausen and indirectly played his trump card, namely threatening to leave the city again, although this time it might have been a vabanque game.

> It would be possible, yes it even seems likely, that the gentlemen administrators were unaware that we employed a large number of

---

[150] Seyffer, *Die Unternehmensgeschichte*, 138.
[151] Report of the Board of Directors of the International Watch Co. in Schaffhausen, business period from 1 January 1874 to 30 June 1875, IWC Archive, DC 05-1000, 9.
[152] König, "The International Watch Company," 56.
[153] Announcement, Jones to the shareholders of the International Watch Comp., Schaffhausen, August 28, 1875, IWC Archive, DC 04-1000.
[154] Ibid., 1.

workers outside Schaffhausen. And bringing these workers here together was one of the main reasons for installing this society and promoting the industry in this city.[155]

Jones eventually achieved his aim to dissolve the board, but this success would not last long.[156] The new board included Jones himself, Julien Rauss, who was Jones's right-hand man at the IWC, two other industrialists from the city, as well as three bank directors. Since the American probably needed the goodwill of the latter, he agreed to accept the formation of the so-called Weidlich Commission, which was supposed to provide a detailed audit report for the IWC, the later Weidlich Report.[157]

This report would provide better insight for investors and board members for them to get a better idea of production processes and the company's overall rentability. Considering the results presented, including transparent and exemplary accounting, Seyffer argues that Jones did not fail with his company due to insurmountable economic problems, but rather due to the way he addressed his problems, namely without sufficient consultation with the board and the IWC's investors.[158] Since the internal struggles had been made public, many investors also tried to sell their shares, even if they lost money at this point.[159] On 12 October 1875, an extraordinary board meeting presented the results to the IWC's shareholders, and it was decided that the chef de bureau would no longer be appointed by Jones, although the latter and the shareholders that still backed him could prevent this decision from being carried out. While the public opinion about Jones was quite ambivalent, the shares lost around two-thirds of their value and the pressure on the American intensified.[160] Jones fired 40 workers to reduce costs, but thereby also limited his possibilities of keeping production numbers high. On 4 December, Jones finally ran out of money and could no longer pay anything. A day later, the process to declare insolvency was initiated and it began ten days later, although Jones and Rauss had already left Schaffhausen by then, and the former was residing at the Grand Hotel du Lac in Neuchâtel.[161] The IWC joint-stock company had gone bankrupt after two years, and although Jones might be

---

[155] Ibid., 2.
[156] See *Neues Schaffhauser Intelligenzblatt*, September 2, 1875 and *Tagblatt für Schaffhausen*, September 1, 1875.
[157] Weidlich Report, Schaffhausen, September 24, 1875, IWC Archive, DC 03-2.
[158] Seyffer, *Die Unternehmensgeschichte*, 145.
[159] König, "The International Watch Company," 58.
[160] Ibid., 59.
[161] Seyffer, *Die Unternehmensgeschichte*, 144.

considered a visionary with regard to his production processes, he was unfortunately not a successful businessman and did not think beyond his own universe, which was centered around the idea to transplant the American system of watchmaking into the IWC in Schaffhausen.[162] Without Jones, a new joint-stock company was established and the IWC's history continued.[163] With experts on the new board, including the author of the Weidlich Report,[164] attempts were made to regain some trust and new investors: "With the intention of promoting the watch industry, which includes the International Watch Company, in order to preserve our city, a number of men have initiated the establishment of a stock corporation, and have appointed the signed board of directors at the constitution of the company that took place today."[165]

It was pointed out that incorrect information had been provided in the past and that there had been problems with the centralization of production. The invitation also highlighted that in the past, i.e. under Jones, the IWC had not been run according to good economic practice.[166] However, with the existent inventory, worth ca. CHF 530,000,[167] it would be a missed opportunity not to use the chance to continue watch production in Schaffhausen. There was still a fear that an outsider might buy the company to move it to another place, however. The hope for the IWC to become a successful part of the Swiss watch industry was consequently still alive, although Jones's behavior must have damaged the dream of the investors in Schaffhausen quite a bit. Nevertheless, the IWC stayed alive and production eventually continued after it was re-established as another joint-stock company.[168] Jones, however, would no longer be part of it and returned to the United States.

---

[162] Ibid., 147.
[163] Statutes of the International Watch Company in Schaffhausen 1876, IWC Archive, DC 02-1000.
[164] Ibid., 16.
[165] Invitation to Sign Shares of the International Watch Company in Schaffhausen, April 12, 1876, StdA SH, D III 02.16/05, 1.
[166] Ibid., 1-2.
[167] Ibid., 2.
[168] IWC, Protocols of the Creditor Committee, StdA SH, County court, CIII 01.02.06.05-018.

Conclusion

When Jones left Switzerland, the era of the IWC was still only beginning, and the company celebrated its 150th anniversary in 2018 with special watch designs to celebrate its long history.[1] While the company's history successfully continued, Jones had to abandon his dream of his own watch company and would not return to the watch production business before his death in 1916. It is assumed, however, that he worked as a dealer in New York until 1883, although he does not appear in US tax records during the 1870s and 1880s.[2] Later, he is mentioned in tax documents as a "manufacturer and developer of steam piping systems, chiefly for use in central-heating installations,"[3] obviously in relation to his employment at the American Steam Appliance Co. That he never really lost his interest in watches and did not quit his work as an inventor completely can also be documented by some patents he registered between 1883 and 1907 for clockwork mechanisms, as well as control elements that were used for cash registers.[4] In 1882, Jones married Susan Prescott Jones from Kingston, New Hampshire, but they would have no children. Jones eventually died on 18 October 1916, and his death certificate mentions "Paget's disease, acute ascending spinal paralysis, [and] lobar pneumonia" as the causes of death for the man who then lived at 43 Adams Street, Sommerville, Massachusetts.[5] His corpse was later cremated at Mount Auburn Cemetery in Cambridge, Massachusetts, but there is no grave for Jones there. His ashes must have been taken home by his wife, and ultimately, the only place to commemorate Jones and his legacy might be the IWC factory building in Schaffhausen.

---

[1] Tracey Llewellyn and Adi Soon, "IWC's '150 Years' Jubilee Collection," *Revolution*, August 17, 2018. Accessed December 1, 2020. https://www.revolution.watch/iwcs-150-years-jubilee-collection/.
[2] Seyffer, "Watchmaking," 25; Tölke and King, *IWC*, 18.
[3] Seyffer, "Watchmaking," 25.
[4] Ibid.
[5] Extract from Records of Death, City of Sommerville, Massachusetts, April 3, 1917, IWC Archive DC 04-26/28.

Fig. 1: Mount Auburn Cemetery, Cambridge, Massachusetts. Photograph by Frank Jacob.

Considering the initial question of the present book of whether Jones was a kind of con-artist, a daring individual who acted alone, or a representative of a larger American network of investors, I think one can answer it by saying that he was all three things, although not always at the same time. I would like to explain this evaluation, having now presented the known facts about Jones's history in relation to the US Civil War, the American watch trade, and his venture in Switzerland, in some more detail here.

Conclusion 89

Fig. 2: Mount Auburn Cemetery, Cambridge, Massachusetts.
Photograph by Frank Jacob.

Of course, Jones was not a classic con-artist, but with regard to his final perception by his Swiss investors, he might have left that impression, especially since he did not share all his information with the shareholders and his business partners. I think he did this because he feared losing control over his dream. Jones wanted to run the IWC alone, without interference, and according to his own vision. In that sense, he was probably too inexperienced as a businessman to see the necessity for trust between inventor and investor. However, it was not only Jones who wanted to sell his dream, even if he did not display it as accurately as possible all the time. It was also the investors who wanted to believe in this dream, especially since the financial elite of Schaffhausen were interested in gaining a share of the Swiss watch trade in the second half of the 19th century.

Jones was definitely a young and daring individual who would take the risk of transplanting a production procedure from the United States to Switzerland, and in this regard he was definitely and without any doubt successful, since the American system of watchmaking allowed him to produce a relatively high quantity of quality watches. Frankly speaking, it took guts to go abroad to fulfill a vision, and although the world was already quite globalized at that time, Jones's attempt was definitely bold. The fact that Jones did not continue working in a different watch company after his return to the United States, in contrast to Kidder, is also an aspect that might point to the direction that he acted as an individual, but maybe he had just fallen out of favor with the American watch industry as he must have cost some people quite a lot of money.

Fig. 3: Mount Auburn Cemetery, Cambridge, Massachusetts. Photograph by Frank Jacob. Unfortunately unrelated to Florentine A. Jones.

Conclusion

And it is ultimately the aspect of money that makes it hard to believe that Jones acted on his own. He must have had investors in the United States, who probably also helped him to become a member of a lodge in Washington. How would Jones have otherwise been able to do that and why would he have needed it if he did not plan to use the masonic network for economic purposes? This, nevertheless, should not create a conspiracy-like narrative about Jones, but the fact that he never communicated the financial aspects of his business makes it hard to reconstruct a network that backed him, at least in the initial period after his move to Switzerland. This, however, also does not mean that such a network did not exist at all. Jones's position and his contact with many other men in the watch business, including Dennison, at least give the impression that Jones had powerful contacts in the United States who were supporting his plans. That he named movements after his uncle Craig might be a hint at the right direction here, but without additional sources that unfortunately are yet to come to light, it will be impossible to make a final judgment on this matter.

Both personally and according to the existent sources and works about Jones, I think that all three named identities were in place at different times between 1867 and 1876. Regardless of this assumption, with which the reader might, of course, disagree, it is safe to say that Jones's history is intriguing, and although he failed, the lasting success of the IWC in Schaffhausen proves that his vision was important. Just as important were his endurance and the fact that Jones did not give up on his dream easily. He endured, but a lack of capital and his personal behavior toward investors and banks made it hard for others to keep faith in his vision. Like many other inventors, Jones eventually failed with regard to the economic aspects of his business, and his failure is in this regard no exception. Many inventors, like the ones in the initial period of the industrialization of American watchmaking in the 1840s, failed to leave a legacy that would continue to live long afterward. Jones must therefore be honored for his role in the initial period of the globalization of the American system of watchmaking and with regard to Swiss economic history in general and the history of the city of Schaffhausen in particular. He is an example of the dictum that those who dare drive history forward.

Works Cited

Archival Sources

City Archive Schaffhausen, Switzerland (Statdarchiv Schaffhausen, StdA SH)
Bildersammlung, Strassen A-Z, 13/40
Bro 1242
C II.58.33/001
D III 02.16/03
D III 02.16/05.
Population register, N3, No. 1501-3866
RRA 2/7297

IWC Archives, Schaffhausen, Switzerland
DC01-1002
DC02-1000
DC03-2
DC 04-26/28
DC 04-27
DC04-1000
DC05-1000
DM05-1151

New England Historic Genealogical Society
Massachusetts, Mason Membership Cards, 1733-1990

State Archive Kanton Schaffhausen (STASH)
RRRA 2/7297.

The National Museum of American History, Archives Center, Washington, D.C.
Collection No. 776: E. Howard Clock Co. Records

Journals and Periodicals

Chicago Tribune
L'Exposition universelle de 1867: Publication internationale autorisée par la Commission impériale
Neues Schaffhauser Intelligenzblatt
Tageblatt für den Kanton Schaffhausen
Tagblatt für Schaffhausen
The Jewelers' Circular and Horological Review

The Watchmaker and Jeweller

Secondary Works Cited

Abbott, Henry G. *History of the American Waltham Watch Company of Waltham, Mass.* Exeter, NH: Adams Brown Co., 1968.

Abbott, Henry G. *The Watch Factories of America: Past and Present.* Chicago: Geo. K. Hazlitt & Co., 1888.

Adkin, Mark. *The Gettysburg Companion: The Complete Guide to America's Most Famous Battle.* Mechanicsburg, PA: Stackpole Books, 2008.

Ahlenius, Jason. "Sensation's Imperial Narratives: Affect in the United States' Democracy of Print, 1846–1848." *Western American Literature* 50, no. 4 (2016): 285-315.

Anderson, Benedict. *Imagined Communities. Reflections on the Origin and Spread of Nationalism.* London: Verso, 1983.

"A Peek at the Past… Florentine Ariosto Jones," *Rumney Historical Society,* June 20, 2018. Accessed October 1, 2019. http://rumneyhs.blogspot.com/2018/06/a-peek-at-passt-florentine-ariosto-jones.html?view=magazine.

Bailey, Chris H. *Two Hundred Years of American Clocks and Watches.* Englewood Cliffs, NJ: Prentice-Hall, 1975.

Balsiger, Roger Nicholas. *Heinrich Moser (1805–1874): Internationaler Uhrenfabrikant, visionärer Industriepionier.* Zurich: Verein für wirtschaftshistorische Studien, 2007.

Barreyre, Nicolas. "The Politics of Economic Crises: The Panic of 1873, the End of Reconstruction, and the Realignment of American Politics." *Journal of the Gilded Age and Progressive Era* 10, no. 4 (2011): 403-423.

Bentley, Thomas. *The Illustrated Catalogue of the Centennial Exhibition, Philadelphia, 1876.* New York: John Filmer, 1876.

Bernergger, Michael. "Die Schweiz und die Weltwirtschaft." In *Die Schweiz in der Weltwirtschaft (15.-20. Jh.).* Zurich: Chronos, 1990.

Berner, Georges-Albert and Emil Audétat. *Schweizer Pioniere der Wirtschaft und Technik,* vol 13. Zurich: Verein für Wirtschaftshistorische Studien, 1962.

Blanchard, Philippe. *L'établissage: Étude historique d'un système de production horloger en Suisse (1750-1950).* Chézard-Saint-Martin: Editions de la Chatière, 2011.

Blind, Adolf. *Die Heimarbeit in der Schweiz.* Jena: Fischer 1929.

Boillat, Johann, Anton Näf and Peter Hans Horn. "Jules Grossmann: Ein Eberswalder Uhrmacher in der Schweiz." *Eberswalder Jahrbuch* 26 (2018): 98-105.

"Born of a Dream." Accessed November 1, 2020. https://www.bornofadream.com/.

Buchheim, Christoph. *Industrielle Revolutionen: Langfristige Wirtschaftsentwicklung in Grossbritannien, Europa und in Übersee.* Munich: DTV, 1994.

César, Pierre. *Ernest Francillon: Sa vie et son oeuvre.* Saint-Imier: Longines, 1992.

Chapiro, Adolphe. *Jean-Antoine Lépine, horloger (1720-1814): Histoire du développement de l'horlogerie en France, de 1760 à l'Empire.* Paris: Editions de l'amatuer, 1988.

Clark, J.P. *Preparing for War: The Emergence of the Modern U.S. Army, 1815-1917.* Cambridge, MA: Harvard University Press, 2017.

Crossman, Charles S. *A Complete History of Watch and Clock Making in America.* New York: Jewelers' Circular Pub. Co., 1886.

Davidoni, Adriano. "A Short History of Railroad Watches." *Watch Time Middle East*, March 10, 2017. Accessed November 1, 2020. https://watchtime.me/life-style/vintage/article/832/a-short-history-of-railroad-watches.

Davids, Karel. *Dutch Atlantic Connections, 1680-1800: Linking Empires, Bridging Borders.* Leiden: Brill, 2014.

Davies, Hannah Catherine. *Transatlantic Speculations: Globalization and the Panics of 1873.* New York: Columbia University Press, 2018.

Davis, Charles E. *Three Years in the Army: The Story of the Thirteenth Massachusetts Volunteers from July 16, 1861 to August 1, 1864.* Boston: Estes and Lauriat, 1894.

De Fazio, Thomas. "The Nashua Venture and The American Watch Company." *Bulletin of the National Association of Watch and Clock Collectors, Inc.* 17, no. 6 (1975): 574-589.

Dolder, Otto. *Geschichte der Rheinfall-Loge Nr. 9 I.O.O.F. Schaffhausen 1877-1927.* 1927, StdA SH, Bro 1242.

Donzé, Fernand. "Les Jürgensen, horlogers négociants, mécènes, notables loclois: Jules-Frédéric, dit Jules I (1808-1877), Jules-Frédéric-Urban, dit Jules II (1837-1894)." *Biographies neuchâteloises* 3 (2001): 218-222.

Donzé, Pierre-Yves. *Histoire de l'industrie horlogère suisse: De Jacques David à Nicolas Hayek (1850-2000).* Neuchâtel: Ed. Alphil, 2009.

Donzé, Pierre-Yves. *History of the Swiss Watch Industry: From Jacques David to Nicolas Hayek.* Bern: Peter Lang, 2015.

Donzé, Pierre-Yves. "Industrial Leadership and the Long-Lasting Competitiveness of the Swiss Watch Industry." In *Historians on Leadership and Strategy: Case Studies From Antiquity to Modernity,* ed. Martin Gutmann, 171-191. Cham: Springer, 2019.

Donzé, Pierre-Yves. *Industrial Development, Technology Transfer, and Global Competition: A History of the Japanese Watch Industry since 1850.* London: Routledge, 2017.

Donzé, Pierre-Yves and Shigehiro Nishimura, eds. *Organizing Global Technology Flows: Institutions, Actors, and Processes.* London: Routledge, 2013.

Eckhardt, George H. *United States Clock and Watch Patents, 1790-1890: The Record of a Century of American Horology and Enterprise.* New York: n.p., 1960.

Fallet, Estelle and Alain Cortat. *Apprendre l'horlogerie dans le Montagnes neuchâteloises, 1740-1810.* La Chaux-de-Fonds: Institut l'Homme et le Temps, 2001.

Fallet, Estelle, Musée Rath et al., *Watchmaking in Geneva: The Magic of Craftsmanship.* Geneva: Musées d'art et d'histoire, 2011.

Favre-Perret, Edouard. *Rapport présenté au haut conseil fédéral sur l'industrie de l'horlogerie: Exposition de Philadelphie, 1876, Section Suisse, Groupe XXV.* Winterthur: Westfehling 1877.

"Florentine Ariosto Jones," June 30, 2015. Accessed September 15, 2019. https://www.iwc.com/de/de/articles/experiences/florentine-ariosto-jones.html.

Freimaurerloge Akazia, ed. *200 Jahre Freimaurerloge Akazia Winterthur*. Winterthur: K-Edition, 2020.

Friedberg, Michael. "F. A. Jones: The Man and the Mystery." Accessed December 1, 2020. https://www.iwc.com/ch/en/forum/the-man-and-the-mystery.html.

Gallagher, Gary W. ed. *The Fredericksburg Campaign: Decision on the Rappahannock*. Chapel Hill, NC: University of North Carolina Press, 1995.

Giauque, Laurent, Vincent Guggisberg and Christian Milz. *Longines*, 2. vols. Neuchâtel: [Université de Neuchâtel Division économique et sociale, 1988.

Goldberger, John. *Omega Watches*. Bologna: Damiani, 2005.

Graham, Martin F. and George F. Skoch. *Mine Run: A Campaign of Lost Opportunities, October 21, 1863–May 1, 1864*. Lynchburg, VA: H. E. Howard, 1987.

Grassias, Ivan et al. *Sur les traces de l'empire Japy*. Salins-les-Bains: Musées des techniques et cultures comtoises, 2001.

Guelzo, Allen C. *Gettysburg: The Last Invasion*. New York: Knopf, 2013.

Hancock, David. *The Sea in History: The Early Modern World*. Woodbridge: Boydell Press, 2017.

Hansen, Peter A. "Still Controversial: The Pacific Railroad at 150." *Railroad History* 208 (2013): 8-35.

Harrold, Michael C. *American Watchmaking: A Technical History of the American Watch Industry 1850-193*. Columbia, PA: National Association of Watch and Clock Collectors, Inc., 1984.

Hauser, Albert. *Schweizerische Wirtschafts- und Sozialgeschichte*. Erlenbach-Zürich/Stuttgart: Eugen Rentsch Verlag, 1961.

Henderson, William D. *The Road to Bristoe Station: Campaigning with Lee and Meade, August 1–October 20, 1863*. Lynchburg, VA: H. E. Howard, 1987.

Hennessy, John J. *Return to Bull Run: The Campaign and Battle of Second Manassas*. New York: Simon & Schuster, 1993.

"Henri Robert Ekegren." *Le Point*. Accessed December 1, 2020. https://www.lepoint.fr/montres/Magazine/Grand-horlogers/henri-robert-ekegren-03-12-2012-2018111_2978.php.

Hess, Earl. *In the Trenches at Petersburg: Field Fortifications and Confederate Defeat*. Chapel Hill, NC: The University of North Carolina Press, 2009.

"History." *Harvard College Observatory*. Accessed November 2, 2020. https://hco.cfa.harvard.edu/history.

Hoke, Donald. "Ingenious Yankees: The Rise of the American System of Manufactures in the Private Sector." *Business and Economic History* 14 (1985): 223-235.

Hoke, Donald R. *Ingenious Yankees: The Rise of the American System of Manufactures in the Private Sector*. New York: Columbia University Press, 1990.

Hoover, Gary. "Battle of the Giant Watchmakers." *American Business History Center*, September 25, 2020. Accessed November 1, 2020. https://americanbusinesshistory.org/battle-of-the-giant-watchmakers/.

Hounshell, David A. *From the American System to Mass Production, 1800-1932: The Development of Manufacturing Technology in the United States.* Baltimore: Johns Hopkins University Press, 1984.

Jacob, Frank and Gilmar Visoni-Alonzo. *The Military Revolution in Early Modern Europe: A Revision.* London: Palgrave Macmillan, 2016.

Jacob, Frank and Mario Keßler. "Transatlantic Radicalism: A Short Introduction." In *Transatlantic Radicalism: Socialist and Anarchist Exchanges in the 19th and 20th Centuries,* eds. Frank Jacob and Mario Keßler, 1-20. Liverpool: Liverpool University Press, 2021.

Jacob, Frank and Martina Kaller. "Introduction: Commodity Trade, Globalization, and the Making of the Atlantic World." In *Transatlantic Trade and Global Cultural Transfers since 1492: More than Commodities,* eds. Martina Kaller and Frank Jacob, 1-12. London/New York: Routledge, 2019.

Jürgensen, Jules-Frederick-Urban. *De l'emploi des machines en horlogerie: Speécialement dans la fabrication des montres de poche.* Neuchâtel: Wolfrath et Metzner, 1877.

Kaplan, Lawrence S. "Jefferson, the Napoleonic Wars, and the Balance of Power." *William and Mary Quarterly* 14, no. 2 (1957): 196-217.

Keller, Theo. *Schweizerische Industrie-Gesellschaft, Neuhausen am Rheinfall, 1853-1953.* Neuhausen am Rheinfall: SIG, 1953.

Klooster, Wim and Gert Oostindie. *Realm between Empires: The Second Dutch Atlantic, 1680-1815.* Ithaca, NY: Cornell University Press, 2018.

Knoepfli, Adrian. "Eine Schaffhauser Gründung im Allgäu: Die Baumwollspinnerei Wangen (1859-1992)." *Schaffhauser Beiträge* 78 (2004): 239-298.

Koller, Christophe. *L'industrialisation et l'état au pays de l'horlogerie: Contribution à l'histoire économique et sociale d'une région suisse* (Courrendlin: Editions Communication jurassienne et européenne (CJE), 2003).

König, Thomas. "The International Watch Company of New York, from 1872-1874." In David Seyffer, Thomas König and Alan Myers, *F. A. Jones: His Life, Legacy and Watches,* 30-61. Schaffhausen: IWC, 2013.

Krick, Robert K. *Stonewall Jackson at Cedar Mountain.* Chapel Hill, NC: University of North Carolina Press, 1990.

Lamard, Pierre. *Frédéric Japy et son héritage.* Belfort: Société belfortaine d'émulation, 1999.

Linder, Patrick. *Longines, un sablier et des ailes: Histoire, enjeux, construction d'une marque: 120 ans de la protection d'un logotype (1889-2009).* Saint-Imier: Editions des Longines, 2009.

Llewellyn, Tracey and Adi Soon. "IWC's '150 Years' Jubilee Collection." *Revolution,* August 17, 2018. Accessed December 1, 2020. https://www.revolution.watch/iwcs-150-years-jubilee-collection/.

Lorenz, Jacob. *Die wirtschaftlichen und sozialen Verhältnisse in der schweiz. Heimarbeit: mit besonderer Berücksichtigung der Ergebnisse der schweizerischen Heimarbeit-Ausstellung.* Zurich: Kommissionsverlag der Buchhandlung des Schweiz. Grütlivereins, 1911.

Lossing, Beson J. *Mount Vernon and Its Associations: Historical, Biographical, and Pictoral.* New York: Townsend, 1859.

Marti, Laurence. *L'émergence du monde ouvrier en Suisse au XIXe siècle* (Neuchâtel: Suisse Editions Livreo-Alphil, 2019).

Martin, David G. *The Second Bull Run Campaign: July–August 1862*. New York: Da Capo Press, 1997.

Marx, Karl. *Das Kapital*, vol. 1. Hamburg: Otto Meissner, 1867.

Meacham, John. *Thomas Jefferson: The Art of Power*. New York: Random House, 2013.

McCrossen, Alexis. *Marking Modern Times: A History of Clocks, Watches, and Other Timekeepers in American Life*. Chicago/London: The University of Chicago Press, 2013.

McCrossen, Alexis. "The 'Very Delicate Construction' of Pocket Watches and Time Consciousness in the Nineteenth-Century United States." *Winterthur Portfolio* 44, no. 1 (2010): 1-30.

Moore, Charles W. *Timing a Century: History of the Waltham Watch Company*. Cambridge, MA: Harvard University Press, 2014 [1945].

Moser, Heinrich. *Die Förderung einheimischer Industrie durch Wasserbauten im Rhein betreffend, zwischen der Stadtgemeinde Schaffhausen einerseits, und Hernn Heinrich Moser auf Charlottenfels, anderseits*. Schaffhausen: Murbach & Dechslin, 1861.

Muir, Diana. *Reflections in Bullough's Pond: Economy and Ecosystem in New England*. Hanover, NH: University of New England Press, 2000.

Muir, William. "The Problem of Chestnut Street." *Bulletin of the National Association of Watch & Clock Collectors* 13, no. 11 (1969): 1019-1021.

Myers, Alan. "Construction and Development of the F.A. Jones Watch." In David Seyffer, Thomas König and Alan Myers, *F. A. Jones: His Life, Legacy and Watches*. Schaffhausen: IWC, 2013.

Nijssen, Gerrit. "E. Howard & Company." *Bulletin of the NAWCC* 36, no. 292 (1994): 563-593.

Nosworthy, Brent. *The Bloody Crucible of Courage: Fighting Methods and Combat Experience of the Civil War*. New York: Carroll & Graf, 2003.

O'Reilly, Francis Augustín. *The Fredericksburg Campaign: Winter War on the Rappahannock*. Baton Rouge, LA: Louisiana State University Press, 2003.

Pfaff, Adam. *Heinrich Moser: Ein Lebensbild*. Schaffhausen: Verlag der Brodtmann'schen Buchhandlung, 1875.

Pfister, Ulrich. "Die Entstehung des industriellen Unternehmertums in der Schweiz, 18.-19. Jahrhundert." *Zeitschrift für Unternehmensgeschichte* 43 (1997): 14-38.

Pöhlmann, Klaus. "Edouard Koehn: Über eine Uhr auf seiner Spur." *Klassik Uhren* 20, no. 1 (1997): 26-33.

Priestley, Philip T. *Aaron Lufkin Dennison: An Industrial Pioneer and His Legacy*. Columbia, PA: National Association of Watch and Clock Collectors, 2009.

"Railroad Industry." In *The New Encyclopedia of Southern Culture, vol. 11: Agriculture and Industry*, ed. John F. Stover, 317-319. Chapel Hill, NC: University of North Carolina Press, 2008.

Rheker, Dirk. "Auf den Spuren des Gründers." *Watch International: Das Uhrenmagazin der IWC Schaffhausen* 1 (April 2008): 27-33.

Richon, Marco. *Omega: The History of a Great Brand.* Bienne: Omega SA, 1994.
Roberts, Kenneth D. and Snowden Taylor. *Eli Terry and the Connecticut Shelf Clock*, second edition. Fitzwilliam, NH: Ken Roberts Publishing Company, 1994.
Ruh, Max. "Ein Amerikaner als Schaffhauser Industriepionier." *Schaffhauser Magazin* 3 (1992): 41.
Sachs, Jeffrey D. *The Ages of Globalization: Geography, Technology, and Institutions.* New York: Columbia University Press, 2020.
Salon international de la haute horlogerie. *La haute horlogerie genevoise, des origines au Poinçon de Genève de 1886.* Geneva: Salon international de la haute horlogerie, 2011.
Schreck, Martin. "Die gewerbliche und kunstgewerbliche Heimarbeit in den Gebirgsgegenden der Schweiz und die mit ihr zusammenhängende Produktion für den eigenen Bedarf." Dissertation Thesis, University of Bern, 1957.
Schivelbusch, Wolfgang. *Geschichte der Eisenbahnreise: Zur Industrialisierung von Raum und Zeit im 19. Jahrhundert*, seventh edition. Frankfurt am Main: Fischer, 2000.
Shelley, Frederick. *Early American Tower Clocks: Surviving American Tower Clocks from 1726-1870.* Columbia, PA: National Association of Watch and Clock Collectors, 1999.
Seyffer, David. *Die Unternehmensgeschichte von IWC Schaffhausen: Ein Schweizer Uhrenhersteller zwischen Innovation und Tradition*, 2 vols. Ober-hausen: Athena, 2014.
Seyffer, David. "Innovation oder Nachahmung? Überlegungen zur Einführung des American System of Watch Making in der Schweiz Ende des 19. Jahrhunderts." In *Alles nur geklaut? Innovationsfähigkeit im Kontext von Technologietransfer und Industriespionage*, eds. Thomas Schuetz and David Seyffer, 9-26. Stuttgart: IZKT, 2018.
Seyffer, David. "Watchmaking in the 19th Century." In David Seyffer, Thomas König and Alan Myers, *F. A. Jones: His Life, Legacy and Watches*, 6-29. Schaffhausen: IWC, 2013.
Sigmond, Aaron. *Bulova: A History of Firsts.* New York: Assouline Publishing, 2017.
Späth-Walter, Markus and Historischer Verein des Kantons Schaffhausen. *Schaffhauser Kantonsgeschichte des 19. und 20. Jahrhunderts*, vol. 1. Schaffhausen: Meier, 2002.
Spörri, Rudolf. "Rheinfall-Loge Nr.9 Schaffhausen." In *100 Jahre Odd-Fellow-Orden in der Schweiz 1871-1971*, ed. Oskar Glaus, 115-119. Wimmis: Odd-Fellow-Bund, 1971.
Stephens, Charlene E. *On Time: How America Has Learned to Live by the Clock.* Boston: Bulfinch Press Book, 2002.
Strum, Harvey. "Rhode Island and the Embargo of 1807." *Rhode Island History* 52, no 2 (1994): 58-67.
Tellis, Gerard J. and Stav Rosenzweig. *How Transformative Innovations Shaped the Rise of Nations: From Ancient Rome to Modern America.* London: Anthem Press, 2018.
Tölke, Hans F. and Jürgen King. *IWC: International Watch Co. Schaffhausen.* Zurich: Verlag Ineichen, 1987.

van Wickeren, Alexander. *Wissensräume im Wandel: Eine Geschichte der deutsch-französischen Tabakforschunng (1780-1870)*. Cologne: Böhlau, 2020.

Visitors' Guide to the Centennial Exhibition and Philadelphia. Philadelphia: J.B. Lippincott & Co., 1876.

von Holtey, Georg, Ursula Bischof Scherer and Albert Kägi. *Deutschschweizer Uhrmachermeister und ihre Werke vom 14. bis 19. Jahrhundert*. La Chaux-de-Fonds: Chronométrophilia, 2006.

Vouga, Frédérique et al. *Les Jürgensen*. Neuchâtel: Nouvelle revue neuchâleloise, 1996.

Wangsrichanalai, Kanisorn. "Battle of Cedar Mountain." *Encyclopedia Virginia*, January 12, 2016. Accessed November 10, 2020. http://www.Encyclopedia Virginia.org/Cedar_Mountain_Battle_of.

Wenzlhuemer, Roland. *Connecting the Nineteenth-Century World: The Telegraph and Globalization*. Cambridge: Cambridge University Press, 2012.

Zeuske, Michael. *Schwarze Karibik: Sklaven, Sklavereikulturen und Emanzipation*. Zurich: Rotpunktverlag, 2004.

Index

A

abandoned 7, 49, 57, 79
Abbott, Henry G. 7
advantage 24, 26, 45, 51, 70
agent xii, 65, 68
Akazia 42
  see also lodge
ambitious xx, 18, 20, 53
America 1, 4, 57, 68, 81
American
  investors xvi, 63-4
  market xi-xii, xix-xx, 5, 37, 45, 64, 78
  standards xiii, xviii, 58
  system of watchmaking xi, xiii, xvi-xvii, xxi, 1, 17-18, 21, 24, 26, 34-5, 45-6, 48, 51-6, 58-9, 62, 67-8, 82, 85, 89, 91
Appleton
  Robbins & 78
  Tracy, & Co. 22
assets 4, 55, 63, 65, 83
attractive 29, 71, 75
authorities 13, 49, 54, 76

B

bank 57, 73-6, 81, 84
bankrupt 18, 21, 24, 26, 34-5, 37, 75, 84
battle 39
birth 29, 61n71
Biver, Jean-Claude 46
board 75-6, 78, 80-5
  IWC's xi, xiv-xvi, xx-xxi, 57
Bond, William C. 13-14
business xi, xviii, 74-6, 78-9, 81-3, 87, 89, 91
businessman 18-20, 60, 74, 82, 85, 89

C

calculation 72, 75, 77
capital xix, 5, 7-8, 18, 37, 41, 54-5, 57, 63, 67, 70-2, 74-6, 83, 91
catalog 64, 68
century 1, 3-4, 8-9, 11, 13, 17, 24, 26, 46, 48-9, 52-4, 55n41
cheap 2, 12, 15-17, 36-7, 41, 43, 47, 51-3, 58, 60
chef de bureau 76, 84
Chicago 41, 62
city 14, 38, 47, 54, 56-61, 64, 66, 71, 74-6, 93-5, 91
Civil War, The *see* war
class 3, 11, 17, 31, 54n41
clock 6, 13-14, 16, 38, 71
  see also watch
colleagues 3, 5
combat 39
combination 14, 24, 26, 35, 78, 82
commission 79, 81, 84
companies 11, 17-18, 24, 26-8, 34-8, 46, 54, 58-60, 64, 79
  see also watch companies
company *see* watch company
competition 17-18, 35, 38, 46, 59
con-artist 88-9
conservative xi, 45, 54

construction 62, 76, 78
consumer 17, 24, 35
corporation 64-5, 85
cottage workers 49
country 8, 10, 21, 30, 32, 37, 53-4, 57, 59
craftmanship 59
crisis 55, 78, 80
customers 3, 8-13, 15, 24, 29-30, 34, 51-2, 68

D

Davis, David 20
dealer 42-3, 59, 79, 87
debts 34, 73, 75, 82-3
decision xii, xvi, 45, 59, 74, 76, 84
demand xiii, 3, 7, 13, 16, 18, 21, 26, 29-30, 32, 34, 44, 47, 51-2, 55, 59, 76, 78, 83
Dennison, Aaron Lufkin 18.23, 40-1, 45, 59, 64, 91
Dennison Standard Gauge 18-19
design 7, 21, 24, 26, 67
determined xvi, 8-10, 18, 38
development i, xvii, 1, 11, 17-18, 20, 24, 26, 30, 37, 45-7, 50, 53-4, 60, 78-9, 83
display 9, 11, 17, 32, 89
dollar 17
dominated 4, 32, 46
dream 41, 45, 54, 59-60, 68, 72, 74-5, 82, 85

E

economic xiii, 11- 17-18, 49, 53, 60, 78, 84-5
economy 53
elite 60, 62, 89
emigration 57
energy 58, 60 83

England 4-5, 7, 20-1, 41, 49, 64
English 2, 4-5, 17, 20-2, 24, 26, 32, 37, 82
English-style 24-6
engraved 32, 62, 70
essential xvii, 1-2, 21, 24, 26, 29-31, 49, 53, 58, 60
establishment xix, xx, 28, 37, 51, 63, 65, 71, 79, 85
euphoria 41, 60, 72
Europe ix, 2, 4-5, 34, 42, 45, 47, 52, 58
European 5, 15, 17, 52-3
experience 28-29n2, 37, 45, 51, 60, 74, 83
experiments 12, 66
export 4, 47-9, 52-3, 55, 68-9

F

factory building 64, 67, 72, 75-6, 78, 83, 87
see also watch factory
failure xvii, xxi, 35, 45, 91
family xiii-xiv, 38, 66
financial xvii, 11, 24, 26, 55, 57, 63, 65, 73-6, 78, 81-3, 89, 91
France 4, 7, 47
Francillon, Ernest 46
French 3, 47-8, 60, 82
fresh
  loans 82
  money 75
  see also capital
fulfill 24, 26, 60, 74, 81, 89
future 21, 29-30, 49, 57, 74-6, 78

G

Geneva 46-7, 49, 59
Goddard, Luther 4-5
globalized xiii, xix, 21, 51, 53, 89

gold 13, 30, 51, 79
Gold, John 21
Great Britain 13
group 21, 24, 26, 42, 65, 74
growing 5, 8, 10, 12-13, 16-18, 23, 30
guild 47, 49, 53, 57

H

Harrold, Michael C. 1, 17-18, 20, 24, 32
high-quality xi, xvii, xviii, xxi, 37, 45, 53, 72
highlight 21, 42, 53, 67
history 1, 37, 59, 87-8, 91
   see also International Watch Company
home xviii, 13, 30, 39, 46-7, 49, 52, 59, 73, 87
   workers 46-7, 49, 52, 58, 60, 74, 81
hope xi, 38, 60, 82, 85
Howard, Edward 8, 20-4 26, 28, 40-1, 43, 58, 71
human xiii, 9, 57
hunter 67, 69
hybrid 22, 68
hydroelectric power 76, 78

I

idea xi-xii, xix, xxi, 5, 7, 19-20, 29, 37-8, 40-1, 43, 45, 58-9, 70, 76, 84-5
imported 4-5, 20, 22, 35, 41, 52
income 17, 34, 52, 63
individual 5-6, 9, 32, 44, 63, 88-90
industrialization 5, 8, 53, 56-7, 91
industrialized xix, 7, 24, 26, 54, 60, 81

information xiv, xvi, 13, 20-1, 85, 89
innovations 9, 49
innovative 19, 34, 37, 49, 56, 70, 83
intensive xii, 7, 15, 30, 35, 41, 63
interchangeable 6, 19, 45
interest 6, 8 10, 12, 22, 28, 30, 47, 49, 64, 68, 75-6, 81, 87
international xvii, xx, 7, 48-9, 51, 53, 55n46, 60, 72
International Business Machines (IBM) 11
International Watch Company (IWC) xi, xv, xx, 38, 41, 45, 52, 64-5, 68, 74, 85
history of 53-4, 73, 85
inventor 6, 7, 21, 23, 24, 26, 82, 87, 89, 91
investment xv, 41, 53, 63, 74, 82
investors xv, xvi, 8, 21, 26, 34, 41-2, 44, 55, 57-60, 62-5, 71-2, 74-6, 78, 82-5, 88-9, 91

J

Jerome, Chancey 16
jeweled 17, 36
jewelers 7-8, 11, 16, 26, 30, 34, 37, 42, 46, 58, 64, 68
joint-stock 64-6, 71, 74-6, 84-5
Jurgensen, Jules F.U. 52

K

key-wind 67, 69-70
Kidder, Charles L. 62-3, 90
knowledge xiii, xv, xviii, xxi, 5, 8, 20-1, 24, 26, 28-30, 37, 55, 68, 82

L

labor xii, xviii-xix, xxi, 18, 29, 34, 37, 41, 46, 51-4, 57, 59, 68
 division of 18, 46, 49-50, 53
law 64-5
legacy xv, 56, 59, 87, 91
life xiii-xvi, 9-10, 23, 38, 45
loan 75, 80, 82
local 4, 8-9, 13, 38, 53-4, 57, 60, 68, 74
lodge 42-3, 62, 91
 see also masonic

M

machines xvii, xii, 6, 18-20, 45, 54, 56, 63, 72, 75
machinery 34, 48, 55, 62-3, 68, 70
management xvii, 3, 7, 10, 22, 53, 82
manufacturers 4-5, 17, 22, 34-5, 37, 49, 51-4
manufacturing xvii, xviii, 3, 35, 46-7, 53, 60, 79
market xii, xviii, xxi, 2, 4, 8, 15, 17-18, 20-1, 22, 32, 35, 37-8, 41, 48, 51, 53, 55, 58, 60, 72, 78-9, 82
 American xi-xii, xix-xx, 5, 37, 45, 64, 78
 US xii, xv, 17, 38, 41, 78, 81
masonic 42-3, 91
 see also lodge; Akazia
McCrossen, Alexis 9, 31
mechanized xviii, 18, 71, 81
memorabilia 30
metal 60, 79
methods xii-xiii, xxi, 5-7, 18-21, 23, 46, 48, 54, 81
migration 56
military xvii, 6, 29-30, 38-40, 55

models xviii, 10, 21, 23-4, 37, 54, 78, 81
modern xxi, 1, 3, 5, 7, 9-11, 20, 30, 37, 39-40, 67, 72, 76
modernity 11
money xii, xv, xvi, 21, 34, 41, 45, 52, 56-7, 62-3, 66-7, 74-6, 78, 82, 84, 90-1
Moser Dam 58
Moser, Henry 60-2, 75
Myers, Alan 70

N

Napoleonic Wars 5
narrative 91
Nashua Watch Co. 24, 26
nation 4, 8-9, 30, 32, 53
national 8-10, 13, 30, 32, 41
necessities 3, 9, 24, 26, 82
network xv, 41, 44, 46, 49, 64, 82, 88, 91
New England 13
nickel 36, 67

O

ocean xiii, 2
operations 61, 76
opportunity 59, 85
origin 7
outsourcing 41
output 6-7, 21, 55, 76, 78, 80-1

P

Patek Philippe 16
payment 65, 79
peddlers 15
pension 38
people xi, xiii, xiv, xvi-xvii, 5-6, 8-9, 11, 1417, 20, 24, 26, 29, 32, 34-5,

Index

49, 53-4, 57-9, 64, 68, 71, 74-5, 90
period 18, 24, 26, 28, 41, 58, 61-3, 65-6, 78, 81, 91
personal 5, 10, 32, 37, 91
phenomenon 18, 29
Philadelphia Centennial Expedition 24, 26, 37, 52, 55-6
pioneers xii, xv-xvi, xviii, xxi, 1, 7, 18, 24, 56, 59, 67
Pitkin 7, 19
pneumonia 87
pocket watch 8, 13, 21, 24, 29-32, 34, 52, 70, 73
    watches xvii-xviii, 3, 8-11, 22, 29-30, 32, 35, 51-2, 55n46, 56, 70
political xiiin10, 8, 53
popular xii, 22, 30, 38
portfolio 68,71, 78, 81, 83
position xxi, 8, 52, 75-6, 91
power 8, 21, 60, 76, 78
precise 9-11, 14, 24, 26, 40, 56
precision xii, xvii, 10, 36
President 5, 74
price xi, xviii, 11, 17, 22, 37-8, 41, 43, 52, 78, 80
problem 7, 20, 52, 67, 73, 76-7, 81
product, 7, 24, 29, 34, 46-8, 51, 66-7, 78-9
production xvi, 1, 6, 11-12, 15, 17-21, 23, 26, 34, 37-8, 40-3, 46-56, 65-7, 70-2, 74, 76, 78-81, 83-5, 87, 89
    industrial xii, xvii, xxi, 7, 45, 60, 62
    mass 11-12, 17, 51, 54, 63, 68
    process xvii-xix, 7, 19-21, 24, 26, 43, 51-2, 55, 58-9, 63, 67, 70
    system xix, 4, 7, 46, 52, 56, 62, 68

progress 29, 53
prominent 14, 42
promise xvii, 18, 75
proprietor 66, 75
property 76, 83
prototypes 21, 62
public 8-11, 13, 22, 57, 74, 83-4

Q

quality xi-xiii, xvii, 24, 26, 31, 37, 40, 45, 51-3,63, 68, 72, 89
quantity 24, 26, 35, 40, 89

R

railroad 30
raw movements 47-9, 51, 69, 72, 78
recession 18, 21
records 38, 40, 87
recruited 58, 62, 64, 74
region 57, 60, 62, 74
regime 8-10
regiment 38-9
relationship 9, 32, 62, 76, 78
reorganized 22
replace xvii, 35, 74
representative 44, 55n46, 81, 88
research xvii, 1, 7, 17-18, 20, 24, 26, 37
resources 1, 49, 53, 60
result xi, xiii, 7, 21
retail 13
revolution 18
Royal Robbins 21-2
rural 8-9, 30

S

sabotaging 83,

sales xvii, xx, 7, 12, 18, 21, 32, 51, 67-9, 78, 80-1
salesman xv, 18
secure 7, 17, 51, 62, 75, 82
segment xviii, 11, 17
service xvii, 13, 30, 39-40
Seyffer, David xi-xii, xvi, xviii, xxi, 38-9, 61, 63, 72, 84
Shaffhausen waterworks 76, 58, 63
shareholders 64-5, 81, 84, 89
similar xv, 3, 6, 19, 34, 37, 42, 49, 53, 55, 63, 72
single xvi, 13, 44, 49, 51, 54, 79
skeptical 54, 81
skills 5, 20, 28, 37, 41, 55-6
small xiii, 47, 53, 62, 68, 71, 81
soldiers xvii, 29-32, 39
specialized 51-2, 59, 71
standard 8, 11, 13-14, 26, 68
status 11, 17, 31
steam engine 76, 78
Stratton, Nelson P. 19, 21
stubborn xviii, 82
success xi, xviii, 1, 5, 11-12, 21, 29, 32, 35, 41, 45-6, 49, 57, 64, 70, 72, 75, 78, 83-4, 91
successful xx-xxi, 1, 5, 37, 40, 49-50, 53, 65-6, 68, 75, 82, 85, 89
suffer 24, 26, 34, 38, 72
Superintendent 20, 40, 68
support 2, 35, 41-2, 57-8, 62, 74, 76, 82
survive 7, 38, 51, 63
Switzerland 32, 41-9, 51-61, 63-5, 67, 73, 75, 78, 81, 87-9, 91
Swiss xi-xii, xviii-xix, xxi, 7, 18, 32, 37, 41-2, 44-5, 48-9, 51-2, 55-60, 63-5, 68, 71-6, 80, 85, 89-91

T

technical xvii, 82

technological 4, 9, 14, 17, 49, 54-5, 82
technology xvii, xxi, 1, 13, 30, 49, 55, 62, 72
telegraph 13
textile business 53
Thomas, Seth 8
timekeepers 36
timepieces xi, xvii, 3, 5, 9, 37, 45
tower clocks 8-9
traditional xi, xviii-xix, 6, 16, 45, 55
train xvii, 11, 62-3, 66-7, 83
transantlantic xii-xiii, xvii, 5, 15, 21
transition xxi, 1, 54-6
Tremont Watch Co. 32, 34, 41, 59
trouble 21, 78-9, 81

U

uniform xiv, 14, 50
union 30-1, 57
unjeweled 36
US-Mexican War 29

V

value 5, 23, 55, 57, 83-4
variety xxi, 26, 51, 66
venture 44-5, 53, 61, 63-4, 68, 75, 88
Virginia 39, 79
vision xviii, 74, 89, 91
visionary xx-xxi, 82, 85

W

Waltham 20, 22-6, 35, 78-80
war xiii-xix, xvii-xix, 18, 28-32, 34-5, 37-41, 43, 45, 52, 59, 73, 78, 88

Index

watch
- business 4, 6, 8, 37, 41, 44, 53-4, 59, 62, 91
- companies xx, 5, 20, 26, 28, 30, 32, 34, 36-7, 41, 54, 63, 73, 78
- company xv, xvii-xviii, xxi, 5, 11, 20-4, 26, 32, 35, 37-8, 40-1, 45-6, 56-9, 62-3, 65, 75
  - American 5, 23, 76
  - Boston 5, 21-4, 26
  - Waltham 20, 23-4, 26, 35
- factory iv, xii, xv, xviii, 7-8, 21, 35, 40-1, 47, 51-2, 55-6, 60, 62, 64, 66-7, 72, 74-6, 78, 81, 83
- industry i, xii, xv, xvii-xviii, xxi, 1, 7, 10-11, 18, 29-30, 37-8, 41, 45-6, 49, 54, 56, 60, 85, 90
- movements 26, 41, 59, 64, 67, 69-70, 76, 79
- production 4-5, 8, 11, 18, 20, 35, 37, 49, 51-2, 54-6, 58-9, 64, 67-8, 76, 85, 87
- trade 8, 37, 46-7, 49, 51-4

watches
- demand for 13, 16, 18, 30, 43, 47, 78
- high quality xi, xvii, xxi, 72
- production of xvii, 17, 45, 49, 51-3, 60, 63
- selling 7, 29, 34, 37, 79
- Swiss 17, 37, 42, 50, 52, 58, 80
- quality xi, xiii, xvii-xviii, xxi, 5, 18, 63, 68, 72, 89

watchmaking xi-xii, xvi-xvii, xii, 1-2, 7, 17-18, 21-2, 24, 26, 34-5, 38, 40, 45-9, 51-9, 62, 67-8, 82, 85, 89, 91
- American xiii, xvi, xviii, 5, 24, 26, 28-9, 74, 91
- Swiss xix, 24, 26, 45-6, 49-50, 53, 56-7

Weidlich Commission 84
wholesale 13, 16, 35
Willard brothers, the 11-12
wine 42-3, 57
Winterthur, 42, 60, 73-6
women 58, 71, 73
work xi, xiii, 5, 20-1, 42, 45, 48, 51, 55, 68, 70-1, 74, 78, 87
workers xiii, xix, 21, 34-5, 37, 44, 51-2, 55, 57, 59-60, 62-3, 83-4
workforce xviii, 35, 51, 54, 59, 71, 74
worldwide 41, 52, 73

Y

young 42, 46, 59, 61, 67, 72, 74, 82, 89

Z

Zürich 60, 76

www.ingramcontent.com/pod-product-compliance
Lightning Source LLC
Chambersburg PA
CBHW070303230426
43664CB00014B/2617